THE FRENCH
AND THE REPUBLIC

The French and the Republic

BY CHARLES MORAZÉ

Translated by Jean-Jacques Demorest

KENNIKAT PRESS
Port Washington, N. Y./London

THE FRENCH AND THE REPUBLIC

Les Francais et la Republique
© 1956 by Max Leclerc et Cie, Proprietors
of Librairie Armand Colin
English translation © 1958 by Cornell University
Reissued in 1972 by Kennikat Press by
arrangement with Cornell University Press
Library of Congress Catalog Card No: 75-153260
ISBN 0-8046-1578-0

Manufactured by Taylor Publishing Company   Dallas, Texas

Preface

PROFESSOR CHARLES MORAZÉ wrote his book, *The French and the Republic*,[1] early in 1956, during the "crisis" which saw the elections of a new National Assembly, the formation of a Republican Front government, the break between Mendès-France and the Socialists, and the beginning of the Mollet government. It was a time of stress, of frustrated hopes, of lost opportunities—one bound to call forth on the part of the friends of France gloomy reflections about the country's future. But it was not a time of "unexpected" developments. Indeed, most of what happened then, or since, can be described as inevitable. The reader of this book will say that the paradoxes of French policy, the recent dramatic turn of events, can all be explained. And he will say as well that the revolutionary expectations of Morazé have been prophetic.

This short essay does not belong to the already too long series of books attempting to portray France as a misguided child, as an incorrigible nation straying from the obvious and clearly marked path of common sense and duty. What Morazé does first of all is to re-establish a sense of history and continuity. We are not allowed to forget that as a national entity France

[1] *Les Français et la République* (Paris, 1956). Five copies of the original French edition were printed on special paper for presentation to Charles de Gaulle.

PREFACE

is very old indeed and that the present can therefore be best explained in terms of the past. The French have a sensitive memory. The debates of today take place within a frame of reference that was established long ago, and contemporary events are seen in all their subtleties and nuances. Logic does not mean simplification.

Morazé refreshes our recollections concerning some of the permanent characteristics of the French people. One of them is the extraordinary intellectual brilliance of the French mind, its inventiveness and technological imagination, its ability to build systems and to create the most astonishing prototypes both of ideas and of the instruments of our industrial society. Coupled with this creativity in the realm of theory we find, according to Morazé, a notable reluctance and caution when it comes to translating ideas into practice. Mass production too seldom follows the prototype. The invention is left on paper. Morazé has some thought-provoking, even though faintly paradoxical and bitter, passages on the cleverness with which the British, borrowing carefully saved French gold, have in the past built modern factories with it and, having returned the gold, engaged the French in ruinous competition.

The lag between theory and practice, between inventiveness and industrialization, is explained in part by Morazé in terms of the unusual problems that France has had to face. The matching of material resources and human skills and of mines and transportation and markets, the finding of adequate sources of raw materials, have been possible only after endeavors of particular difficulty and have tended to discourage and blunt the investments needed for economic development.

One of the most attractive features of Morazé's book is the very large canvas on which, with bold strokes, dazzling (and for cautious readers perhaps startling) paradoxes, and most imaginative parallels, he paints the history of France in relation to the other great powers. France is the conscience of the world, the mirror which reflects its tensions and crises. If too

PREFACE

many of his arguments appear to have economic overtones, Morazé's justification is that the industrial revolution of the last 150 years has produced more upsetting results, has had more drastic repercussions, than any other event in the history of modern civilization. And the difficulties that France has been experiencing have often been due to the troubles she has had in adapting herself to the exigencies of large-scale output.

But the book makes clear, too, that the French crisis flows from the particularly wide gap between the conditions imposed by the scientific revolution of our times and the age-old residues of forms and structures that France is reluctant to give up.

Morazé is aware of the exposed situation of France in the great tug-of-war that separates East from West and of the problems the country has to face in coping with the Soviet Union. No one can forget that dangers to freedom and democratic institutions can come from the fascist Right as well as from the Communist Left. In dealing with the duties of tomorrow and in painting a seemingly unduly complicated and baffling picture, in inducing some sobering reflections on the policy requirements of the West, Morazé performs a useful task.

This is a tract for the times. Written in the midst of the 1956 crisis, it is published in the United States in the midst of the French crisis of 1958. It is a polemical book, one sometimes extreme in its positions, but wonderfully helpful in making us understand the tragedy of France, a country that seems at last to be coming into her rightful economic inheritance through scientific progress, industrial renovation, and discovery in the Sahara of great natural resources, while the institutions of the Fourth Republic are crumbling.

Morazé tells us that if the Sahara belongs to anyone, surely the title deeds of France cannot be forgotten. Uninhabited, without visible resources, isolated, the desert is being trans-

PREFACE

formed by French daring and persistence, skills and investments. And on the eve of reaping the legitimate fruits of her sacrifices, France may run the risk of being cut off from it by the surrounding hostile Arab lands, which she has deeply wounded and with which she has so far been unable to come to any agreement.

These are the tensions and the fears at the origin of the national drive, the pride, the extremity of solutions, that appear to be the normal way of expression for the French people and French governments. It is in forcing our attention away from forms and institutions and procedures to the underlying social and economic factors, to the scientific and industrial revolutions under way, to the broad horizons that, for the first time in the twentieth century, are perhaps within the reach of France, that Morazé performs his most significant service for all those who are confused by the course of events in the country Americans like to call their oldest ally.

This is a book for the imaginative and perceptive student. As it raises France from the morass of its postwar vicissitudes, it gives us a vision of hope for the future.

I wish to express my gratitude to Professor Morazé for the concluding chapter written especially for this American edition. I also wish to thank my colleague Jean-Jacques Demorest for an admirable translation.

MARIO EINAUDI

Ithaca, New York
May 1958

Contents

Preface iii
Introduction 3

Part One
POLITICAL PSYCHOANALYSIS OF FRANCE

I Preliminary Reflections 17
II The Passion for Theory 20
III The Economic Phobia 32
IV Malthusianism and the Taste for Luxury 49
V Adventurous Courage 63
VI Political Insecurity 76

Part Two
THE DIFFICULTIES OF THE PRESENT

VII French Power in Tow 93
VIII From Provisional Government to Chance Government 120
IX The European Question 134
X Drama Overseas 146
XI Education at a Standstill 157

CONTENTS

Part Three
FRANCE'S DESTINY THE WORLD'S DESTINY

XII	France, the World's Crossroads	165
XIII	The Advance of Progress: The North Atlantic	173
XIV	The Accidents of Progress: Eastern Continents and Southern Seas	182
XV	France, Strength and Weakness of the World	197
XVI	Conclusion	205

Illustrations

1. Urban and Rural Populations in the U.S. and Various European Countries — 36
2. Iron and Coal Deposits in France; Tendency toward the Right; Tendency toward the Left — 38–39
3. Location of French Industry about 1780 — 40
4. Location of French Industry about 1880 — 41
5. Location of French Industry about 1930 — 42
6. The French and the English in North America (17th Century), India (18th Century), and Africa (19th Century) — 70
7. Dominating Traits of the Five Major French Political Tendencies — 79
8. Abstentions from Voting in 1928; Railways about 1848 — 100
9. Abstentions from Voting in 1956; Income about 1954 — 102
10. Communists in 1928 and 1956 — 104
11. Mouvement Républicain Populaire (MRP) in 1946 and 1956 — 106
12. The Radicals in 1928 and the Radicals plus the Union Démocratique et Socialiste de la Résistance in 1956 — 108
13. Socialists in 1928 and 1956 — 110

ILLUSTRATIONS

14. Rassemblement du Peuple Français (RPF) in 1951; Communist Gains and Losses, 1951–1956   112
15. The Right and Poujade, 1956; Increases in Revenue   114
16. The Governments of the Fourth Republic   117–119
17. Radical Votes and Abstentions in 1928; Socialist Votes and Abstentions in 1956   193
18. The Socialisms   200
19. Christian Democratic Movements   201
20. Dictatorships   202

Introduction

IN France, governments do not govern: they reign, they educate. Occasionally they acknowledge the inevitable by means of laws and decrees. They appear all the more active, all the more energetic when they offer little resistance to the pressure of events; at least, their role at such moments is characterized by intelligence and clarity of purpose. But, very rapidly, internal contradictions arise to block the machine as long as the situation will permit; then, the pressure mounting once again, a new mass of legislation is voted upon by the very elements which were most opposed to it.

It does not seem that French assemblies are made to command. Rather they are schools where a candidate to power learns how to administer the nation according to the dictates of external events.

The gap between what candidates to power propose and what events impose explains the fragility of French governments. No matter how intensive the lessons that external events bestow on deputies and senators, they only give them competence over a small number of problems. Once events themselves have imposed a solution, governments are frequently faced with unexpected predicaments that catch them off guard. There then appears but one way out: as rapidly as feasible a new team is sent in.

Now this is the rule in the most favorable cases. In less favorable ones the government itself becomes a sort of school.

French statesmen learn their trade through exposure to it. A peculiar situation, indeed, when one realizes that France requires a thorough culture proved by degrees and endless competitive examinations of all its servants, but not of its statesmen. When it is a matter of government, there is no need to worry: all requirements are dropped. Anglo-Saxon countries are more exacting and their parties have a more rigorous recruitment process. In Russia, the call to government is obviously preceded by a lengthy education. In France? Nothing of the sort; you learn as you govern. In the most favorable cases, township or *département* administration will serve as an introductory course. Usually a man is initiated to government as he sits in the Cabinet.

On the morrow of the elections of January 2, 1956, the leader of an important French party came out of a private conversation during which he had been asked to participate in the future government. Referring to the crucial Algerian question, he made the following statement: "Very interesting interview with the future Prime Minister. I have learned many things." Now what could such a man have taught his electors? And would not the voters have profited by this precious bit of information that he had just learned if they had had it a few weeks before the elections?

A rather enlightening study could be made of the number of French political figures who have acceded to power, not because they had supported a given policy, but precisely because they had always opposed it. In this weird fashion are majorities created. Although a Socialist, Robert Lacoste can enforce an authoritarian program of military occupation of Algeria in direct opposition to his party's electoral platform; whereas Jacques Soustelle, ever favorable to this program and a follower of General de Gaulle, was not allowed to put it into effect. In like manner, General Koenig gave formal implementation to the Geneva agreement, so contrary to his past opinions, and Marshal Juin to the Declaration of Carthage on Tunisia.

It is not a paradox to assert that in France the act of formulating a policy precludes one's being asked to apply it.

Of course, one is tempted to scoff at this ludicrous situation as unworthy of France's great Cartesian tradition. Our aim here is quite different. We do not seek to criticize (newspapers do enough of that) but to understand or, in other words, to compare with what is done elsewhere and with what has been done in France's past. The comparison with other countries demonstrates that France is not radically different from her neighbors. We would be greatly mistaken to assume that among other nations government is based on foresight. Consequently, we have singled out for analysis half a dozen political attitudes characteristic of France, noting that some were typical of Latin countries and some of Eurasia or of North or South America. Perhaps the incoherence of France's politics is the sum of the world's incoherences. A weakness? Assuredly, but also a measure of greatness.

This sort of incoherence is not a new phenomenon in France. The provisional government born of the socializing revolution of 1848 was convinced that it was the founder of an all-powerful Bank of France and of a Discount Bank that would be a model for capitalistic financial institutions and the indirect founder of the great private railway companies. Could the enthusiastic masses greeting the Popular Front Chamber of Deputies of 1936 have suspected that this very Chamber would carry Pétain, a Marshal of France, to quasi-monarchic power? Could the electors of de Gaulle's Rassemblement du Peuple Français (RPF) suspect that they were bringing to the National Assembly the very men who, after a long opposition, would support first the government of René Mayer, then the government responsible for Dien Bien Phu, and finally the governments that abandoned Indochina while reorienting France's African policy?

Nor are the French parliamentary regimes the only ones to enjoy the privilege of incoherence. When Napoleon III promulgated in 1862 the regulations setting up strict financial controls, he fixed for at least a century administrative rules utterly contrary to his industrial and military plans.

When he was writing his books, so remarkably prophetic in their grasp of history, how could General de Gaulle himself have suspected that he would preside over the only governments in which communism imposed its economic and social innovations, that he would be at the helm when France encountered its first difficulties with the Moslems in Syria and in Lebanon?

While co-operating so actively in instituting various forms of nationalization and socialized medicine, did the Communists themselves ever suspect that they were giving liberalism the new blood it needed for its recovery in the 1950's?

Surprising France! She uses her sons according to her needs, not according to their wishes. She is complex, contradictory, demanding, changing, indifferent, rebellious, pacific to the point of numbness, then bellicose beyond understanding. Within her boundaries the world's contradictions meet. No single power can pretend to command France. France retains the upper hand.

Hence certain types of political studies seem absolutely futile, namely, those that attempt an abstract analysis of the constitutions and the political mechanisms of France. There can be no real understanding without a preliminary study of France herself, of her geography and history. There can be no reform of government without a preceding reform of the life and customs of France. A reform of France's way of life is impossible without changes first occurring in the most varied regions of the world, for they all are nourished by and nourish France.

With or without overseas territories, victorious or vanquished, tranquil or in revolt, France can only be understood on a worldwide scale—not because of some sort of divine decree creating Frenchmen as superior world citizens, but simply because France's geographical position has made of her for centuries, and surely for many years to come, a crossroads open to every wind.

Should the French wish to live the secluded life of the Swiss, they could not do so without crossing the Alps. Even a foreigner living on France's soil is molded by its nature and exposed to the four winds of the world's spirit.

Did the young enthusiasts of the Revolution of 1789 ever expect to march as soldiers through Europe? And the peaceful Frenchmen, who in 1936 applauded the creation of a Ministry of Sports and Leisure, how could they conceive what the world's destiny was preparing for them? The words "France alone," whether pronounced by the Right or the Left, are patently absurd. It is perhaps conceivable that an American, a Russian, a Scandinavian, or an Indian should think in terms of isolation. But France is neither Lille nor Metz, neither Marseilles nor Bordeaux: she is their coexistence. Symbolically enough, Paris is the Concord, a vast crossroads halfway between the Place de la République and the Arc de Triomphe.

All the same, one can hope that the France of today will be torn out of the senile clutch of the seventeenth and eighteenth centuries. One can wish for fewer antique shops and more new houses, for a government that would tire of sitting in glorious Louis XV furniture surrounded by tapestries and royal gilt, for a government that will build for the future and relegate the past to the museums.

Before deciding what should be done, let us understand.

France is not the pleasant, easygoing country one usually imagines. She is often a rugged and always a difficult country. Certain regions, certain social groups, have retained a medieval standard of life (I mean, one typical of the poorest people of the Middle Ages, for there were aspects of great wealth in the life of the Middle Ages). A life of primitive hardness dominated by the vagaries of nature is still that of several million Frenchmen. Yet nearby glitters the exasperating luxury of furniture built as jewelry, custom-made cars, the world's most exquisite food, the most elaborate and exacting fashions. Laboratory and industrial techniques belonging almost to the twenty-first century have sprung up next to an agriculture and crafts reminiscent of the thirteenth century. A religious faith of Cistercian rigor flourishes next to trenchant rationalism. How could such complexities ever support a simple and coherent political regime?

A great majority of Frenchmen have two political souls: that of a citizen who realizes that the state is above all himself, that of a subject who considers that the state is only composed of the others—of the wealthier classes, of the Administration. The citizen accepts sacrifices, at times heavy ones. The subject demands subsidies and protective measures; he revolts if he does not obtain them.

It follows that a deputy, the cornerstone of political power, must give explanations to the citizen while extending promises to the subject. He proposes a general program to the citizen, but he promises the subject to intervene personally in his favor. The average elector acts both as citizen and subject; he plays both cards. So does the deputy. So does the minister.

It is impossible to create coherent parties. Little parties multiply within the infinitely varied framework of discordant programs and promises. A party is no longer a clearly defined school; it is an official program riddled by endless individual promises.

The deputy is often relegated to the role of a broker. How could it be otherwise? He deals with an elector just as fond of equality as of privileges—those privileges which the Old Regime used to call "liberties." How can one expect a coherent government to issue from such a complex electorate?

It has been said that one of the reasons for the success of Poujade's movement was not its promise of a general tax reform, but its procurement of tax advantages for many individuals and corporations. This is scarcely a novelty. And, truly, we must consider it a blessing when this trait becomes so embodied in one party that all others are forced to denounce it.

So there evolves a multiplication of complex parties internally split between their program and their promises. If the accession of a deputy to a minister's post seldom allows him to fulfill his program, it at least allows him to keep some of his promises—hence that very temporary affection which clever politicians show for those ministerial posts that lend themselves to the distribution of patronage and personal favors.

The more individual promises a minister redeems, the smaller his risk in not applying the proposed general program. The accession to power composes all contradictions. The greater the number of successive governments, the greater the number of contradictions resolved. The greater the number of governments, the more deputies become for life *"Monsieur le Ministre"* and the smaller their risks of not being re-elected. We cannot blame deputies for the fact that, deep within her heart, unconsciously, France is still 30 per cent monarchical. The history of France is to blame, and perhaps, too, French education, so burdened by the past.

But let us discard these petty explanations; they cannot account for the whole picture. It is in absolute good faith that ministers unwittingly betray their original programs. And for this reason the frequent change of governments becomes a shining virtue.

Indeed, it is a rare occurrence when political problems are clearly set before the electoral body: republicans vs. Napoleon III, partisans of the Resistance vs. Vichy. Normally, the voter must face a confusing mass of intricate problems creating a multiplicity of platforms. This brings in its wake the possibility of such numerous regroupings of parties that the National Assembly itself, not the voters, must make the choices.

Thus successive assemblies and governments do not propose political solutions typified by strong, clear-cut parties. The deputies most adept in handling the contradictory tendencies of the National Assembly are always the closest to power, those most frequently participating in the governments. Obviously, these men are also the least capable of organizing public opinion along definite lines. The success of a deputy called upon to govern is habitually the cause of extreme bewilderment among his electors. But the same electors are conspicuously flattered by the success of the man they voted for: "Now, there is a vote that was not wasted." Thus reacts the average Frenchman. In the presence of a minister he again becomes a subject. Should the elector have another opportunity to vote for the program of a deputy minister whose stay in power was characterized by conspicuous shifts of position, he immediately votes, not for the ideas, but for the man, for the success.

One easily pardons a deputy for not fulfilling his electoral program if he has been fortunate enough to be called to power. Of course, it often happens that a minister is not re-elected to the National Assembly. Because he was unfaithful to his program? Nothing of the sort; it is far more probable that he was defeated because he failed to honor certain personal promises.

When, after the Liberation, the deputies and senators who voted in favor of Pétain in 1940 were declared ineligible, it was perhaps because there were reasons to fear that the electors would forgive them. After all, there had been other examples of this sort of thing. Had not Lamartine, so sure of his own success, refused to forbid the candidacy of Louis-Napoleon Bonaparte? Wasn't his generous gesture punished by a crushing defeat at the hands of the future Napoleon III? And why was the latter elected? For his program? Certainly not; solely because of his name.

Are there, then, no voters firmly committed to programs?

Yes, but they are found on the extremes, not in the Center, and to the Left rather than to the Right. Among the Conservatives, Catholics may remain Catholics; yet they are far less faithful to the Christian parties than are Catholic voters in Italy, or even in Germany, Holland, or Belgium. During the last fifteen years even French Communists have not been exempt from electoral ups and downs due to the exigencies of the conquest of power.

The most striking example is that of the Socialists. For half a century they bitterly fought capitalism. When the crisis of 1930 carried them to power in 1936, they had the support of all the left. But no sooner were they in power than they practiced orthodox liberalism, a careful monetary orthodoxy that renders all the more stupefying the audacious policies of the British Labour Party some ten years later.

The exigencies of government in France confuse basic issues at the time of elections. In Great Britain the dissolution of Parliament occurs when the problems facing the government attain a sufficient degree of simplification (exceptionally, this was the case in France on May 16, 1877). But, by contrast, the dissolution of the French Parliament in November 1955 was pronounced at the moment of greatest confusion; its result was to call for a vote when the French electorate was at the peak of its confusion.

Among the Communists there were no surprises. On the Right a vacuum had arisen due to the withdrawal of General de Gaulle from active politics. It was filled by a new group quite different from the RPF, Poujade's followers. Pierre Mendès-France's desire to provoke a clear division between Right and Left was only effective in the ranks of his own party. By rallying the Socialists to his point of view, he succeeded in creating the Republican Front, but only by weakening the old inclination of the Radical Party toward the Center. This inclination is so inbred, particularly in southern France, that less than a month after the elections it reappeared as strong as ever. In the meantime the regrouping of the moderates created an important group to the right of Center. Thus, four groups immediately stood out. A fifth one was inevitable: supported by dissident Radicals, by some Social-Republicans (ex-RPF), and by the compact MRP (Mouvement Republicain Populaire), several parties of varying importance met on common grounds. The opposition between an important Left and a strong Right would probably have been realized in the case of a Republican Front majority. This solution having been rejected by Republican Front leaders before the elections took place, the system reverted to its normal dependence on the Center. At this point, we note that if the Center, through the mistakes of the MRP and through the professed desire of Mendès-France to create a split between Right and Left, lost for a while its usual premiership, it at least made a choice between the two tendencies of the Republican Front and, through a seeming paradox, chose to promote its Left wing which was then moving to the right instead of the Right wing which had been edging toward the left.

Does this imply that France has never known anything other than a split into five trends and has never been confronted by a Right and Left choice? Certainly not. This choice was available in 1830, 1848, 1871, 1936, and 1944 —in short, at every crisis. And each one of these changes from Right to Left, from Left to Right, entailed a change of constitutions.

Why? That is what we shall try to answer.

PART ONE

Political Psychoanalysis of France

I

Preliminary Reflections

ARE we warranted in undertaking a political psychoanalysis? Are there events in the youth of a people which determine the characteristics of its adulthood, which may explain its passions or its impotence? Is it possible that past events, whose interpretation and precise occurrence escape the man of action, could be analyzed usefully by the historian? We shall certainly not attempt to answer such imposing questions. Rather we shall state that in the case of a given culture nations have a childhood, a youth, a maturity, a death. For France, a nation defined by the function of techniques which came to full development in the nineteen thirties, childhood is located in the middle of the eighteenth century, youth about 1850, maturity toward the beginning of the twentieth century. Since then, during the last two generations, a new France has been in the making.

We shall study here the France which nurtured us, a nation whose youth lies in the nineteenth century.

In the eighteenth century the population of our very young France was characterized by a demographic pyramid with a vigorous and large base made up of youth.

Toward 1939, however, adult France was represented by an inverted pyramid with a small youthful apex and a large base made up of old people. The low birth rate of the years 1935–1940 was the result of the crippling losses sustained in the First World War by an age group that was already the product of years of low birth rate during the period 1885–1895.

And so, by backward leaps of twenty years, from the great historical shock of the war of 1939–1944 to that of 1914–1918, from the general crisis of the 1890's to the War of 1870, from the crisis of 1848–1852 to that of 1830–1833, we finally reach the years of carefree youth of a mechanically inventive France. It was an ardent youth whose vivaciousness exploded about 1789 to attain its full strength twenty years later when Napoleon reigned over Europe and dreamed of becoming the master of Moscow.

The crises in the birth rate, which occurred every twenty years, are just as much the result of immediately contemporary conditions as they are of demographic processes. Such a peculiar situation was created that in the middle of the twentieth century France still bears the consequences of the Napoleonic Wars. Approximately every twenty years since 1820 France has produced a relatively small generation of young adults (19 to 25 years old); every twenty years its creative energy in all domains of economic, social, and political life has undergone a marked atrophy. This predisposition to crises has regularly brought about catastrophes. Out of seven crises, covering four generations, there is a single exception, the generation of 1890. This date coincides with a strong movement of immigration, with a profound realignment of French society, and with the beginning of the second phase of industrialization (the first phase stemmed from steam power and the railroad, the second from electricity, the automobile, and aviation).

We should immediately underscore the fact that the massive adoption of modern techniques in the 1890's is the only plausible explanation for the material and moral resurgence of France between 1871 and 1914. One may hope that this sincere diagnosis will weaken that common and dangerous myth of an automatic rebirth of France after each crisis. There is no such thing as automatic revival. It can come only through effort, intelligent work, progress, and generosity.

In concluding these preliminary remarks, we must assert, if not the validity of a political psychoanalysis, at least the usefulness of searching for the explanation of many of the aspects of contemporary France in the history of her crises during the nineteenth century. One can consider it probable that the events of the nineteenth century, which are, among others, the causes of our present demographic imbalance, are also the causes, among others, of the present psychological and political imbalance. With this in mind, we shall seek in the history of the nineteenth century, and more particularly in the years of our youth from 1750 to 1850, the crystallization of our characteristics, the chief of which appear to be: a passion for theory, an economic phobia, Malthusianism and a taste for luxury, adventurous courage, and political insecurity.

II

The Passion for Theory

DESCARTES, Montesquieu, Auguste Comte—France excels in theory. Conceived in Germany, developed in Great Britain, the *Manifesto* of Karl Marx came to life in Paris. Ever receptive, France has offered mankind a perfect soil for the sowing of ideas.

This was true even before the Revolution of 1789. France played a major role in the definitive formulation of the dogmas and philosophies of Roman Christianity, just as she did in the expression of modern aesthetics, in the architecture of cathedrals, in the institution of the classic arts. France, that extraordinary crossroads of peoples and passions, that cape of embarkation from the old continents toward the new, is so happily endowed by nature that everything converges on her without submerging her. She enjoys the advantage of a great freedom of choice without enduring things too long. Nothing excessive, nothing immoderate. Western France was an English province; southern France was a province of Rome, of the successive Romes. Although she has participated in all types of cultures, France was the first to give an undeniable unity to these diversities, the first to express herself in a tongue which synthesized all previous attempts at expression in the western areas of the old continents.

The exceptional position of France is the source of her real wealth. For her soil, contrary to an old belief, is not rich. Relatively favored by sedimentary deposits around Paris, it is broken up toward the south by granitic masses. France became poor the moment that economic progress was founded on the possession of deep coal and iron mines. Until 1870, not only were her mines hard or even impossible to exploit, but only with great difficulty were they linked to the natural industrial centers of the country. In no other European country, with the possible exception of Spain, did railroads encounter so many obstacles; nowhere were their finances so unsatisfactory.

Hence a nation proud of being the leader of the West met innumerable obstructions during that decisive century when England, then Germany, succeeded in establishing a prodigious mechanization. These unexpected difficulties, arising from terrain and resources, increased the theoretical bent of the French. Or, rather, they aggravated the situation: the mountains that border France, and that have played an essential filtering role in the nutrition of her human equipment (material, physiological, mental), did not produce rich land. If France was the greatest rural nation during the classical centuries, she owed it more to a happy combination of circumstances and to the patient tenacity of her peasants than to natural wealth.

In truth, the wealth of old rural France was in the relative variety of her regions: one could find a bit of everything everywhere. Such a situation is preferable in elementary economies to that of holding the immense rich plains of eastern Europe. This was true until the eighteenth century, but it became much less favorable in the face of the extensive specializations imposed by the modern epoch, during which railways transformed geography.

This sudden inferiority had the following result: France, possessing in 1750 one of the most astounding intellectual equipments the world has ever known, produced from 1750 to 1880 the most ingenious, the most intricate industrial techniques in the midst of natural conditions patently hostile to technical progress. But her spiritual and technical superiority did not save France from very poor business transactions. In every domain she saw her competitors to the east and to the west succeed. They enriched themselves with less labor and less ingenuity in the same situations in which she was being driven to ruin. For this alone there was reason to revolt against Providence.

France is a country where solemn, bold, and penetrating proclamations flourish—a country where the practical application of these splendid notions is ever difficult and uncertain.

It has often been said, and with a measure of reason, that France is the creator of numerous great inventions, the realization of which she leaves to rival nations (England, the United States, Germany). She is the country of beautiful prototypes which can never successfully be mass produced. We could offer a hundred striking and troublesome examples of this fact in the domains of metallurgy and aviation alone.

Let us examine the question more closely. When the moment is ripe for an invention, it often appears simultaneously in several countries, and it is sheer vanity to pretend that any one country is the original home of an invention. Let us take the least contestable example—the least contestable of France's glories—Pasteur. Clearly, to say that microbiology would not have existed without Pasteur is preposterous; its advent would simply have been delayed a few years.

This self-evident truth does not prevent our stating the basis of French superiority as follows: France formulates the key discoveries before her rivals do. But this aptitude for invention and formulation is not followed by a disposition toward practical application. From this point of view, Great Britain and several other nations have indubitably surpassed France.

And now for the fields that concern us directly—law and politics. There is little doubt that France gave to the Declaration of the Rights of Man and of the Citizen a formulation more brilliant than that of the American Bill of Rights which preceded it. There is little doubt, either, that France's Civil Code was a unique masterpiece. She also excels in drawing up constitutions. Step by step her constitutions have answered the political needs of the nineteenth and twentieth centuries. They long enjoyed the privilege of being widely copied in Europe and, at times, throughout the world. Great Britain has no spectacular modern declaration of rights, no code, no constitution. But she observes the habeas corpus and practices criminal and commercial law and parliamentary government with a concrete pragmatism that generates about her an exemplary feeling of security.

The cause and effect of the superiority of British pragmatism are of a historical nature. In the seventeenth century, while France remained loyal to her absolute monarchy, economic and social conditions allowed Great Britain to open a cycle of technical progress involving the gradual establishment of a modern political and legal regime. In France, absolute monarchy lasted 150 years longer than it did in England; but meanwhile French political writers and thinkers grasped the significance of progress in Great Britain and expressed it with ease and rationalism while completely overlooking the details inherent in the practical difficulties of adaptation. The France of the eighteenth century was a master of theory—not only the France of Montesquieu, but also that enormous society composed of judges, prosecutors, appellees, barristers, solicitors, and bailiffs, whose proliferation Racine had already denounced.

Thus the France of Descartes showed a legalistic temperament the Mediterranean roots of which went deep into the old Roman tradition. For more than a century French political thought was restricted to theorizing and to legal discussion because of the persistence of the old monarchy, a persistence deriving from the relative natural inferiority of France in the commercial and industrial fields.

In many respects the intellectual preparation of France for modern political structures was by then superior to that of Great Britain; yet she lacked experimental knowledge. It is this very freedom of mind, founded on practical inexperience, which accounts for the fact that the representatives of the Constituent Assembly were so trenchant in their settling of every conceivable constitutional problem, while long practice had taught the British to be cautious. France formulates her thought with *éclat*, with splendor—a splendor that has never failed to impress the world, usually somewhat behind France in the domain of intellectual accomplishment.

So France expresses herself in magnificent, absolute terms. When she changes constitutions, the new one is likely to be as peremptory as the one just abolished. This trait has continued well into the middle of the twentieth century. The notion that, after all, constitutional practice is a relative matter, or that customs are more valuable than laws, is abhorrent to the French temperament, which, throughout history, has always cultivated principles.

The same frame of mind is observable in the following phenomenon: the establishment of technical progress in the Western world and the economic upheavals that ensued soon inspired a new discipline, economics. In Great Britain, the new discipline was organized in a relatively subtle and independent manner; its spokesmen drew ideas from the fields of psychology and biology. In France, the subject of economics was subordinated to jurisprudence, and until the middle of our century its teaching was entrusted to law schools completely cut off from history, psychology, and, of course, biology. This attitude has justifiably awakened more anxiety than admiration on the part of the practical-minded Anglo-Saxons.

Whether as a paradox or a legitimate consequence of her frame of mind, France, who accomplished miracles in her Civil Code, was outdistanced by Germany in respect to the Commercial Code and long remained behind in social legislation. Are her men at fault? No, the responsibility lies in the evolution of basic geographic conditions which, to this day, make France a more solidly rural, agricultural nation than a commercial or industrial one.

In France certain principles crystallized at the end of the eighteenth century. They worked themselves so deeply into the nation's fiber that numerous changes during the last 150 years have not erased their mark. We shall insist on one of these principles because of its significant political repercussions. Their legal inclination leads Frenchmen to write precise constitutions; but, moved by a tendency toward the abstract, they distrust political parties. Who can state where the British constitution begins and where it ends?

It is the practical genius of Great Britain which forbids an answer: the organization of two great parties and of a constitutional regime is part of a whole that was empirically elaborated in the seventeenth and eighteenth centuries.

On the other hand, France thinks republican in the limited constitutional field; she thinks monarchical in the "free" domain of political parties.

The idea of parties was alien to the philosophy of eighteenth-century France. It was then associated with the hateful remembrance of bitter religious and civil strife. This revulsion away from the party system is encountered in political psychologies emanating from absolute monarchies. The notion of the party also appeared contrary to the achievement of national unanimity, which the First Republic required in order that it worthily succeed the monarchy. This inclination toward unanimity is the essential psychological basis for what Latin America calls "the moderating power." It is also the motivating force of French parties when in control of the government.

In diplomacy as well, the Frenchman frequently reasons as would a subject asserting his "rights" rather than as a citizen of the world.

We shall not elaborate on that famous axiom, "Perish the colonies rather than a single principle." It is to France's honor and it is certainly responsible for a great part of her influence. Rather we shall note here the sequels of the "War of Civilization and Right."

When the pragmatic Anglo-Saxons were studying the advantages they could draw from the German defeat of 1919, they grew impatient at the lack of assistance given them by Poincaré. The Anglo-Saxons were looking for a workable and, above all, a profitable economic solution; the French were pronouncing a judgment and stipulating rights. There was too much realism in one camp, too little in the other. Finally, by giving ground in concrete matters in order better to defend principles, France lost any lasting benefit from German war reparations.

At the same time she lost the psychological benefit of the victory: veterans felt obliged to assert their rights and continued to do so up to the creation by Vichy of its Veterans' Legion. It is as if the atrocious and prodigious effort imposed by the First World War was being kept alive through the impatient claims of its survivors. Instead of the surge of concrete efforts necessary to the rebuilding of a new France, much energy was consumed making out legal reports intended to fix the detailed account of Germany's debt. And a useless account at that! With Klotz, the Minister of Finance, nearly all of France thought: "Germany will pay"; not a single voice rose to explain how it could be done. Germany would pay because justice demanded it.

People said, "Germany will pay," just as their ancestors had said, "The Court will pay." In the twentieth century France still thinks that the solemn proclamation of a right guarantees its execution. In the United Nations this attitude on France's part constantly stands out as her greatest strength and her greatest weakness. In the name of justice the old France of St. Louis still strives to win by right what her industries and trade are incapable of gaining.

Obviously, this queer obstinacy in living outside the lessons of practical experience is not a purely political phenomenon. Also, it is far from causing drawbacks only. A striking example of its possibilities is the metric system. One hundred and fifty years after its birth the metric system is still in its youth and is gaining ground daily. It stems from a singular case of conceptualization contemporary with the creation of the Civil Code. In it we recognize the thought of the great Legendre and a mark of that Cartesian rationalism so frequently evoked out of place, but here, quite fittingly so.

For a long time England had been moving toward the standardization of weights and measures through the free play of astute commercial practices that gave preference to the most convenient methods, until the day when, industry taking the fore, the present British system was definitely adopted. As in the case of her constitution and her law, Britain's system of measures is the end result of a patient selection among the traditions inherited from the past. In France a theoretical creation, the metric system, was inspired first by the oscillation of the pendulum and then by the length of the meridian—inspired also by the decimal system in spite of the difficulty experienced by small tradesmen in abandoning the usual count by dozens. In the eyes of French theorizers custom did not matter: mathematics and eternal verities dictated the change.

In this instance France broke completely with the past, a past in which the volume of bushels and the length of paces varied with the provinces or the build of individuals. Really adopted in the 1830's, contemporary with the advent of the new industrial civilization, the adoption of the metric system by international commerce is still but partial; in the scientific realm, however, it is complete.

It is equally proper to recall the international prestige of the Institut de France from the moment of its inception. To a higher degree than any other institution it distributed fame and authority to research workers of every nation—even the British, so legitimately proud of their Royal Society, did not disdain its consecration. The Institut was for twenty-five years the scientific parliament of a cosmopolitan world. In principle, it was supposed to act as the scientific counselor of the French government. In this role it rapidly revealed itself inferior to the task which the Royal Society fulfilled perfectly during a greater part of the nineteenth century. Once again the theoretical nature of French studies was at fault.

Even French engineering schools demonstrated this inclination toward theory. This is true of the famous Ecole Polytechnique and of the other great technical institutions. Young British technicians prepare for their work and learn their trade in industry itself. Future French technicians are handed over to professors noted because they totally lack practical training. In truth, this question is not so clear-cut if we scan the nineteenth century; after 1870, for instance, the British recognized the necessity of theoretical instruction. Nevertheless, the fundamental traits remain. By a curious but persistent phenomenon, British and German professors, when seized by a thirst for power, throw themselves into business activities. In France they turn to politics and indulge in the most categorical and theoretical proclamations known to the parliamentary repertory. In this way France owes to the chemist Berthelot much less the discoveries of organic synthesis, of which he claimed to be the author (in reality, a German and Swedish discovery), than the immortal cult of political laicism. In marked contrast, Liebig, the German creator of organic chemistry, acquired wealth before scientific immortality thanks to his soups and his successful ventures in the field of nutritive chemistry.

French polytechnical theory does not stoop to commercial calculation, whereas German and English theoretical studies on rail transportation are laden with bookkeeping details. Obviously, Saint-Simon and his followers did not waste time on such trivial matters. Their "Mediterranean

System" was purely conceptual and it ended up in a religion. The celebrated positivism of Auguste Comte had no room for vulgar accounting; it also ended up in mysticism. The accountant, who in other countries is the pillar of prosperity, is characterized in France as a comical person who gnaws life away in a dingy office.

For the past ten years French public accounts, assuming the resounding epithet of "National," have in feverish haste been trying to gild their pale coat of arms. Alas, for lack of preparation and for lack of understanding of the country's economic life, French national accounts remain unbelievably theoretical. Moreover, the so-called "national accountants" would not be caught associating with the rabble of private accountants, nor, for that matter, with accountants working for nationalized industries. They scarcely realize that these "little" accountants belong to the same world. We should note that the recent promotion of accounting into the sphere of the state's great solar system resembles the current Russian experience far more than the Anglo-Saxon or the German capitalistic experience. (We might add that the technical progress of the czarist regime was accomplished somewhat outside bourgeois accounting practices thanks to adventurous French investments.)

As both public and private administrators, the graduates of the Ecole Polytechnique and of the schools that follow its noble tradition have, from 1820 to our day, generously poured the money of the state and of the taxpayers into the coffers of private enterprise on the condition that business faithfully execute their plans—impeccable plans and the most Cartesian in the world for the simple reason that they do not bother with such details as costs.

In the nineteenth century French railroads were technically the most perfect in the world. In Great Britain railroads made the fortune of private companies, which later equipped the world. In Germany the profits from the railways contributed significantly to Bismarck's building of the army of 1870. In France, on the other hand, after having caused the financial crisis which overthrew Louis Philippe, the railways were at the bottom of the distress which, after 1860, drained the public treasury and undermined the war budget. We shall go back to them farther on.

What power, what world renown, French technology enjoyed in every domain—and even to this day! But how great the price!

Religion, constitutions, systems, sciences, laicism, technology—in all of these France stands out as the world's foremost theoretician.

III

The Economic Phobia

THE passionate attachment to theory and the unquestioned prestige that it has brought France is accompanied by a peculiar awkwardness in practical matters. This is not a recent phenomenon: Descartes refused to consider the subject of society. In the nineteenth century, while British, German, and Russian political thought was inspired by the prodigious development of psychological studies, French political thought remained stubbornly rationalistic. Psychology as studied by France's neighbors moved toward the practice of economics, toward the positive observation of economics. The economics of the French during the nineteenth century (we shall discuss the twentieth century farther on) was divided into two entirely distinct sections: one related to technique, the other to law. Between the two, rivalries and quarrels arose. They agreed, however, in their common scorn for psychology, which really ought to have been a natural bond between them. Comte, the positivist, in spite of striking examples given him by Great Britain and Germany (and even by Italy, another victim of the Roman tradition), linked psychology to biology, absolutely denying it separate existence. Psychology was regarded as the private domain of Alexander Dumas, father and son, of poetry, of art. It was refused any identity as a positive science.

This attitude springs, we believe, from the extreme difficulty encountered in analysis of the French temperament. And one of the capital reasons for this difficulty lies precisely in the varied disappointments which theoretical and technical discoveries foster at the time of their practical application. The French industrialist and businessman acquires an evident inferiority complex, which he refuses, as a consequence, to have analyzed; he even denies its existence. In the nineteenth century Germans and Anglo-Saxons generously bared their financial reports to researchers, economists, or sociologists. In France this is still a rarity. What excuses are given? That technical secrets are involved—a false pretext. In reality Frenchmen feel uncertain wherever accounting is concerned.

What proofs can we advance to support our interpretation? All we need to do is to read the reports of French business executives of the nineteenth century. They were constantly clinging to the state to obtain subsidies, credits, and protection, regulatory and tariff. When a crisis broke out, it was never attributed to poor management but to wholly external causes: labor unrest, plots fomented by rival nations, or systematic sabotage on the part of the government.

There is no ground for retorting that this was an attitude common to capitalists the world over, for bankruptcy in England and Germany was a pitiless process. There no extenuating circumstances were admitted. Economic self-criticism is practiced by her capitalistic rivals with infinitely more rigor than by France. Hence that type of humility characteristic of German and British businessmen when they are in the throes of an economic crisis—a humility which shocks the French and which is rashly interpreted as baseness or hypocrisy put on to hide a devious trick.

And, in fact, the "devious trick" occurs inevitably. Impelled by the very rigor of the system and by the strict observation of the rules of bankruptcy, Germany and Great Britain emerge from depressions rid of their unsound business enterprises. The sound ones, which alone can subsist, enjoy a crushing advantage over French firms fettered both by poor business protected by the state and by the laxity of a Commercial Code whose extreme indulgence contrasts sharply with the severity of the French Civil Code. But are we warranted in underlining this contrast? In reality the Civil Code defends property with such jealousy that it saps the strength of commercial legislation. By 1804 Napoleon I had already been forced to denounce this legal mechanism. During all his life as economist and ruler Napoleon III was obsessed by the problem. Yet neither of them succeeded in remedying the situation.

And so in periods of crisis the French businessman never admits his responsibility. He loudly invokes his inalienable property rights in order to escape the consequence of his own poor management. Let us conclude this cursory discussion with a precise example: British courts refuse to accept any extenuating circumstances for the issuance of checks not backed by adequate funds. Generally, this misdemeanor is not even prosecuted in France. Why prosecute? Too many opportunities are given the delinquent to justify his good faith. And once more the accountant (in this case, the bank) is considered the culprit. Hence that old French distrust of checks.

THE ECONOMIC PHOBIA

In depressions, then, then French businessman steers away from self-criticism. On the contrary, he becomes indignant, angry; he accuses. He takes the state, the workman, and foreigners to task. Frequently, public opinion rallies to his point of view. In Great Britain the cyclic crises of 1828–1830 and 1847–1848 caused bankruptcies that were accepted with resignation. In France they resulted in revolutions that brought to power the very men whom the depression threatened with failure: the lower bourgeoisie, the artisans, and the mortgage-burdened small farmers.

Why does this attitude exist? Because the French industrialist, by comparison with his English, German, or American counterpart, has to bear many inferiorities stemming from the physical nature of France. Communications are more difficult, more costly. French railroads, started nearly at the same time as those of Great Britain and before those of Germany, were completed twenty-five years later because of serious physical handicaps. Transportation costs are higher because of the scattering of French industry during the eighteenth century, when a limited urban concentration was accomplished with difficulty. (This explains the slow development of French cities, which are at least fifty years behind those of neighboring countries; see Figure 1.) The poor localization of mines also complicated matters: the iron mines, running deep and containing great reserves, are unfortunately not situated in the proximity of the surface mines that had been under exploitation in the eighteenth century. Finally, French coal mines have been a sorce of disappointment. About 1860 everyone supposed that the Massif Central would become the iron district of France and would rival the prosperity of the English Midlands. Alas! It was

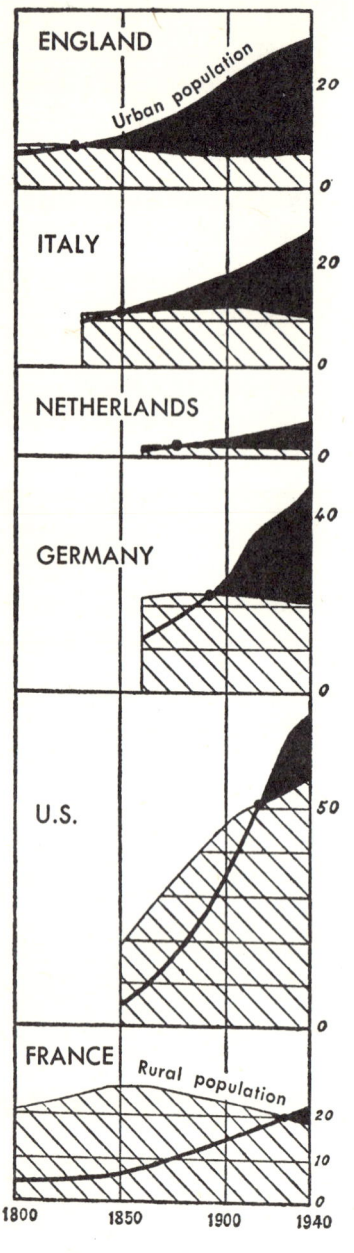

FIGURE 1. Urban and Rural Populations in the U.S. and Various European Countries.

Diagonal lines—rural population in millions; heavy black lines—urban population; all-black areas—excess of urban over rural population.

scarcely started before the exploitation of coal in central France met with the poverty of a substratum that defied profitable extraction. The mines in the North also encountered endless obstacles that account for the series of hardships and failures which were their lot from the beginning of the eighteenth century to the middle of the nineteenth.

Only toward the end of the nineteenth century did French industry find more favorable locations, which were not those of 1860. A whole century was lost in sincere and intelligent efforts, unfortunately betrayed by nature. (See Figures 3–5.)

The anger of capitalists and workmen cruelly victimized in their fruitless efforts was thus partly justified. Bosses and labor alike blamed the state. And until 1880 the state systematically protected management in order not to add the problem of higher wages to the unavoidable physical handicaps. As a result, French social legislation was fifty years behind that of England and Germany. When the British Parliament, about 1840, was voting the Labour Acts, the government of Louis Philippe was sending the army against the workers. In the 1880's Bismarck established the foundations of an efficient system of social security. In France labor legislation came into its own only at the end of the nineteenth century, while French social security did not gain the all-inclusiveness of Germany's until the middle of our century.

Under the circumstances one understands why French workmen invented socialism and revolutionary syndicalism. The difficulties that opposed industrialization being physical, the accession to power of French socialism in 1936 took place much later than it did in Great Britain and, of course, it did so in an atmosphere of tension that

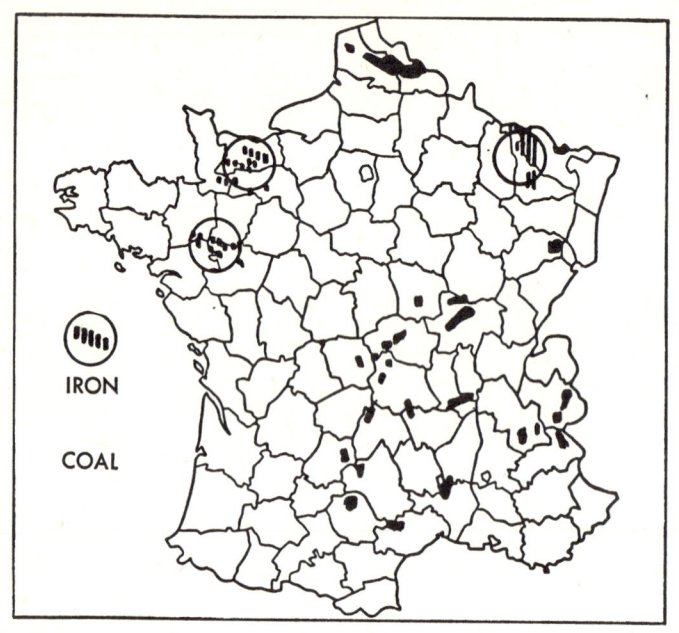

FIGURE 2. Iron and Coal Deposits in France (*above*); Tendency toward the Right (*upper map on facing page*): Tendency toward the Left (*lower map*).

Iron-ore France is rightist France and coal France is leftist France —that is the conclusion to be derived from these three maps. It should be noted that the iron of Brittany has not led to much of an industrial calling but rather to a persistence of the rural economy, while the coal of the Southwest, contrary to the general pattern, has remained bound to a conservative zone. (Maps on p. 39 courtesy of François Goguel.)

THE ECONOMIC PHOBIA

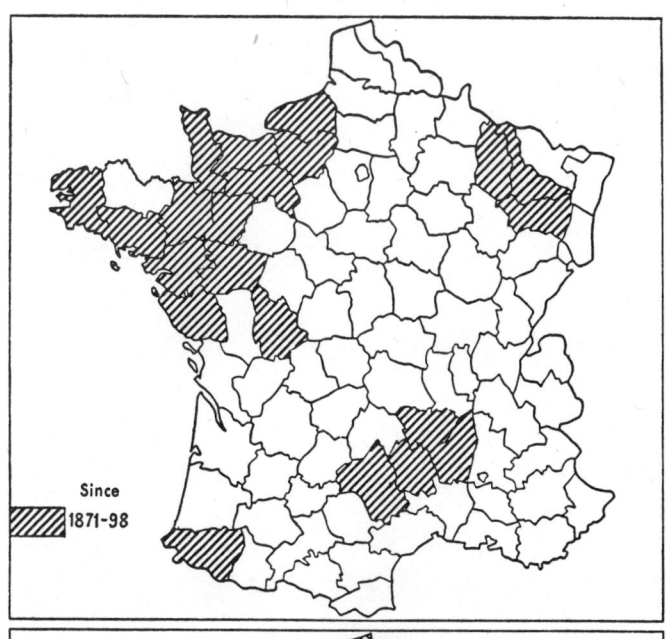

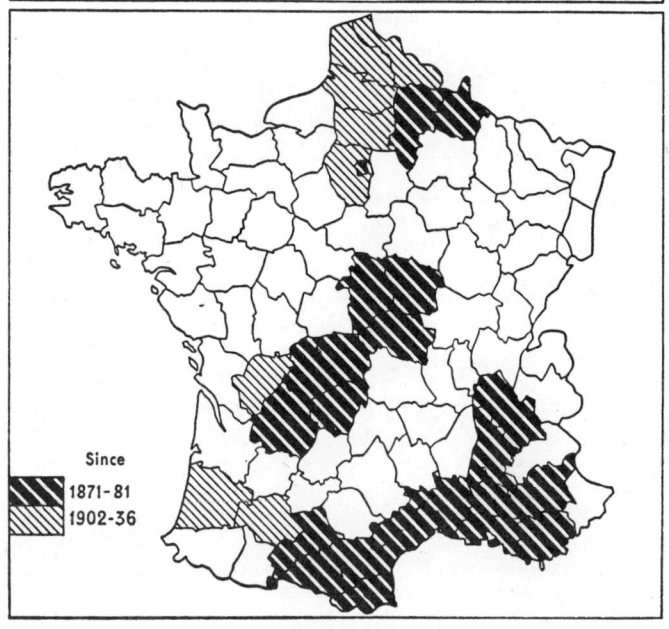

Since
1871-98

Since
1871-81
1902-36

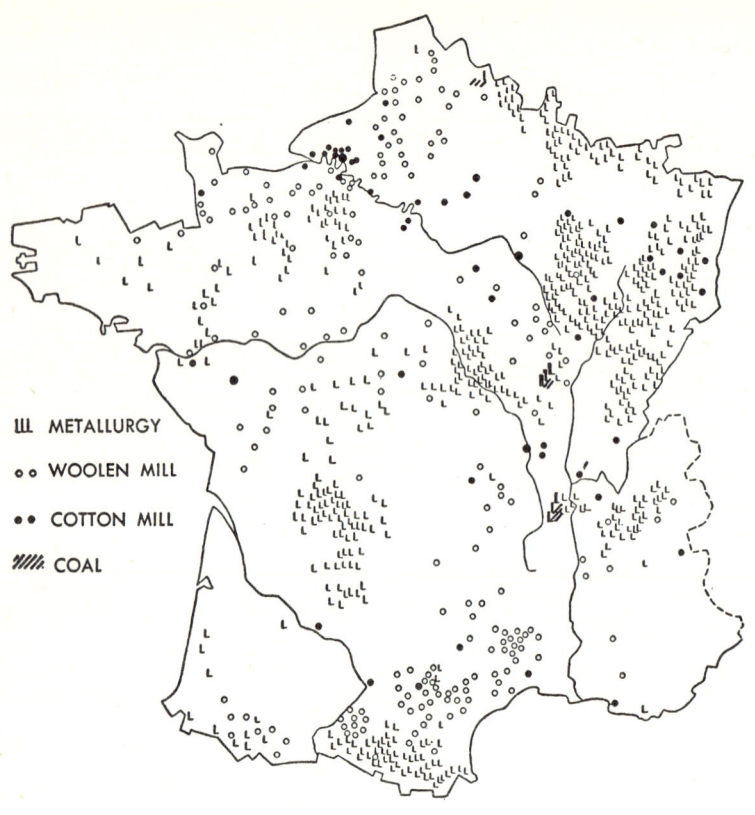

FIGURE 3. Location of French Industry about 1780.

The harmony of the whole picture is striking. Industry is established everywhere, particularly the metallurgical industries. Neither the West nor the South appears in an unfavorable position. And if the East is quite industrial, it is in Champagne rather than in Lorraine.

Coal has made its appearance, but more so around the Massif Central than in the North, where the Ardennes ironworks are more active than those situated in Flanders.

The only North-South opposition is suggested by the textile industry. Cotton, which was at the origin of the great British movement of modernization, penetrated France by way of the coastal rivers, settling more readily in the Northeast and the East than in the South, which remained faithful to wool. Because it is suited to sheep raising, the South is a great center of the wool industry.

This map can be interpreted as a sign that France, especially in the South, is still at the stage of exploiting local resources, whereas England is already industrial because of her trade.

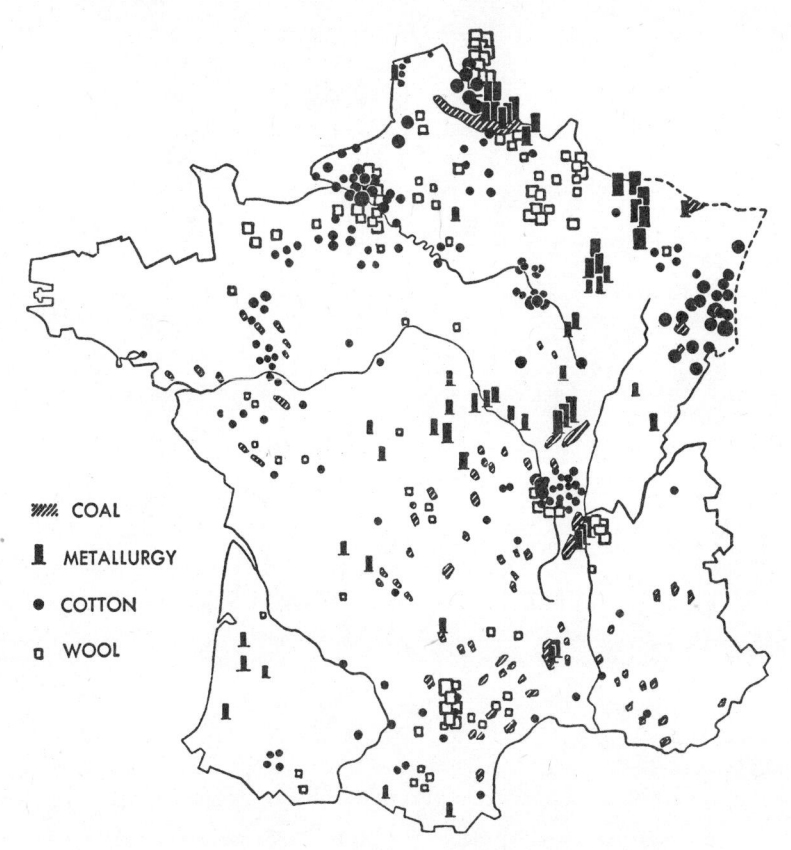

FIGURE 4. Location of French Industry about 1880.

The geographical aspect of French industry about 1880 does not differ much from that of the 1780's. However, centers of crystallization are now evident.

Two types of metallurgy are already apparent: one which has not moved from its traditional location, the other which has settled close to newly developed coal mines. Competition seems to have created a balance between the two. In reality, the former scarcely keeps alive, and the latter is undergoing varying fortunes.

Coal deposits are more numerous in the South and the West than in the North. One is now beginning to realize how poor the southern and western deposits really are.

The textile industry has already migrated northward. In the South it has barely succeeded in holding its own in the Castres-Mazamet region. It is flourishing in Alsace.

The stanch old French tradition of exploiting local resources is revealing itself to be costly. The nineteenth century is associated with a sad story, the failure of raw silk production which French kings since the days of Louis XI had hoped to establish permanently in order to avoid buying silk in the Far East. The fear of great trade has by now proved truly ruinous. The South has lost the textile battle.

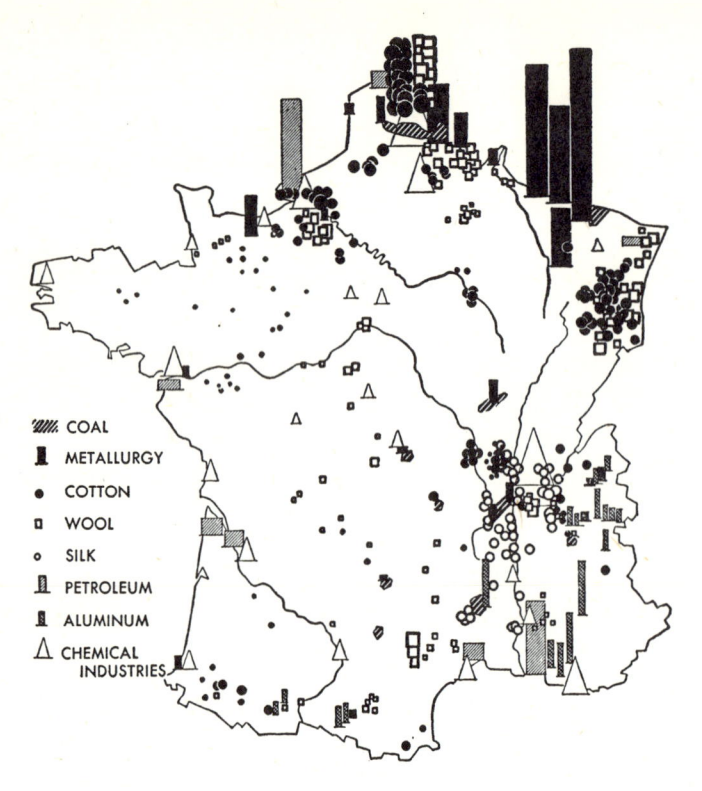

Legend:
- COAL
- METALLURGY
- COTTON
- WOOL
- SILK
- PETROLEUM
- ALUMINUM
- CHEMICAL INDUSTRIES

FIGURE 5. Location of French Industry about 1930.

Heavy industry has died out in the center of France, in Berry and in Champagne. It is in these districts, however, that the first attempts at modernization were made during the nineteenth century. Stagnating, the small coal mines of the Massif Central, the West, and the Southeast have abandoned any hope of supporting heavy industry. Metallurgy has managed to remain in these zones, fixed more by the availability of manpower than by the presence of natural resources.

The southern wool industry has fought fiercely to hold on in Castres, Mazamet, and the Rhone Valley, but it has hardly progressed. The silk industry, partially adopting synthetic fibers, continues to be active in the region of Lyons and the Dauphiné. However, no raw silk is produced locally any more; even the idea has been abandoned.

On the other hand, the industrial resources of the North and the East have proved efficient, and it is there, along the border, that technical progress is the most energetic. Cotton and wool prosper.

Following a similar pattern, bauxite and electricity have created in the Southeast a powerful industry comparable to that concurrently developing across the border in northern Italy.

The chemical production of fertilizers is situated in the rural zones, but the heavy chemical industry is generally located in the North and East. In the meantime, the need for oil has reawakened France's maritime and commercial vocation.

rendered certain urgent tasks impossible of accomplishment.

The insecurity of industrial and urban progress has been one of the permanent traits of France in the nineteenth and twentieth centuries. The astute capitalist has been well aware of this; hence his timidity in developing new industries and his attachment to gold and real estate; hence also his suspicion of bank notes and checks.

In France, the bank note comes a century later than it does in England; the check, fifty years later. Joint-stock companies appear later than in England and Germany. On the other hand, France, which during the eighteenth century was the greatest possessor of gold, has to this day kept her faith in the virtues of gold—all the more so since, for commercial and maritime motives we cannot elaborate on here, the banking efforts of the eighteenth century were nugatory, just as was the financial policy of the French Revolution. (If land seems an ideal investment to the French, it cannot, for technical reasons, usefully replace the bill of exchange in the normal development of fiduciary credit.) The paradox is that during the nineteenth century and, at times, in the twentieth century, the Bank of France, replete with gold, came at every depression to the help of the Bank of England. The latter used French gold to re-equip British factories and ports; at the end of the depression it would courteously repay its debt with interest, so that proud France might once again store away her gold deep in her vaults. Thereupon, the Bank of France would solemnly proclaim that it was the most powerful, the wisest bank in the world. It did so with a vanity that agreeably flattered a public opinion truly delighted to have been asked for help by England. But at that very moment new British products and new British ships, equipped with the help of gold that now slumbered in French coffers, would begin to pour merchandise into French ports. Whereupon the French would vociferate mightily against "perfidious Albion."

France instinctively distrusts an industry that has ups and downs. French capitalism is constantly calling upon the state for help; and its engineers are on the most friendly terms with their old schoolmates from the Ecole Polytechnique, who are in government service. Capitalistic activity clings to the state all the more desperately since, craving gold, the Frenchman has progressively less inclination for financial adventures. When Napoleon founded the Bank of France, he needed a capital of thirty million francs. Inspired by the English example, he perhaps believed that private financiers would furnish the needed capital. Unfortunately, if, in England, the Bank was a private concern lending to the state, in France it was only an apparently private one for which the state had to provide the capital. Napoleon obtained but three million francs from the private beneficiaries of the Bank (those regents whose families were going to dominate French finance for 130 years). The state was obliged to subscribe the remaining twenty-seven millions.

The nineteenth century in France offered little change in financial matters from the seventeenth and eighteenth centuries. No extensive financing was possible except through taxation. Let us go back to the example of the railroads. The liberal state offered to meet the chief construction expenses of private companies and, once constructed, to turn over the whole to private business for the actual exploitation. A royal gift. Yet the companies were hesitant in accepting, and, from 1880 on, roads showing a deficit were generously given back to the state—in particular, the French Western Railway System. Furthermore, once the private business was rid of the heavy responsibility of transportation, it demanded of the state abnormally low transportation rates.

The French industrialist believes the state owes him protection. This unwritten privilege is more tangible than would be a written law. In effect, if it were a law, the right of protection by the state would be in open contradiction with the capitalistic defense of property; and the Cartesian spirit characteristic of the Roman jurist, a spirit which lives in every Frenchman, would wax indignant and resort to a hundred painful arguments. A convenient way was contrived to disguise this contradiction: the right to property was clearly defined, while the state's protection was established vaguely, without really mentioning it.

Without mentioning it? Sometimes a bold fellow dared to. About 1840 the good Guizot, a minister more Anglophile than realistic, thought of imitating his friend Robert Peel and of breaking down tariff barriers: "I certainly hope," exclaimed Mimerel, an industrialist and a deputy, "that the government does not intend to weaken national industry in its control of the country's markets." Quite a formula: extending the right of property to the right of monopolizing the nation's markets! An incredible heresy, but such is the truth; and it couldn't be otherwise. Cobden, an English contemporary of Mimerel, decided to fight with all his might to establish complete freedom of trade. Was this an act of pure generosity? He himself gave the answer: "Let us risk one-half of our fortune to save the rest." Free trade was a vital necessity for Great Britain, just as protectionism was an unavoidable evil for France.

We must render justice to the French. If they do cling to the state, they are also quite willing to entrust it with their savings. The same small capitalists who hesitate to invest in commercial or industrial firms rush to buy state bonds. Just as in the eighteenth century, the state managed to preserve its old monarchical prestige throughout the nineteenth century. To be convinced, all we need to do is read Balzac. And this confidence in the state, not discouraged by devaluations, is still true of France in the middle of our century.

Devaluations? In reality, the capitalist's confidence in the state has, without lasting harm, endured far more grievous disappointments. Thanks to her relative superiority in the world of 1880, France was rich. She was in a position to lend money. Great Britain lent to private companies the world over. The French, however, were suspicious of those joint-stock companies sprouting up in England, America, Hong Kong, or Africa. But let the czar, the powerful czar, deign to ask the French for their gold, and his plea was answered with lightning speed, yes, with mass enthusiasm. France lent great amounts also to the Bulgarian state, the Turkish state, the Romanian state, the Egyptian state. Such is the unbounded prestige of the state in the eyes of the French.

The Frenchman cannot forgive a businessman for endangering his investments. He has never understood the way in which bank failures are settled. An ignorant and suspicious lender, he is the first to demand that the state rescue a bad business in order to safeguard his own investment, regardless of whether such a counterrevolutionary measure compromises the financial soundness of the country and, hence, his own living standards. But the same individual accepts inflation, which is but another way of salvaging bad business ventures.

Whence the torrent of claims immediately after the war of 1914–1918? The undeniable, and undenied, heroism of her soldiers gave France the notion that she had economic rights. She therefore refused to submit once again to the monetary discipline she had endured, with revolutionary outbursts it is true, for a whole century. Since 1919 inflation has reigned, and the French monetary system has been moving away from that of Britain. This was a normal sequel to the deception which followed Germany's inability to meet war reparations. France paid for German insolvency through inflation—in other words, through the ruin of those who loaned money to the state, the money she had hoped to obtain from a defeated Germany.

Since 1919 inflation has been financing the development of power and encouraging technical progress in France. Given the fact that, at the same time, it protects small artisan trades from extinction, it has proved an ideal financial resort for a nation both very modern and very conservative.

Inflation is always unfair to the individual who trusts the state. It is often unfair to the wage earner. But it so readily conciliates the contradictory interests of Malthusian capitalism that it has not permanently injured the credit of the French state. What about monetary orthodoxy? All inefficient business concerns, all sick industries, are opposed to it, and they easily deceive the good public, above all, the good *rentier*. Of course, the desire to save the franc is loudly proclaimed, for who can envisage joyfully the prospect of seeing his savings dwindle? But as for paying the necessary price, in other words, allowing a salutary wave of failures during depressions, that is quite another story! Anything, but not that! And once again inflation plays its role. France accepts the crippling of her own currency, accompanied by the preservation of a multitude of sick and tough "little businesses."

The *citizen*, in a liberal economy, is a man who accepts the risks of the system he lives in; these risks are essentially characterized by business failures.

In economic matters the average Frenchman is a mediocre *citizen*.

The *subject* expects the state to protect his rights, his property; just as, for centuries, the monarchic state protected the interests of trade guilds by special regulations.

In economic matters, the average Frenchman remains a *subject*.

IV

Malthusianism and the Taste for Luxury

IN the first half of the nineteenth century the death rate dropped in France and Great Britain. The birth rate remained comparatively strong in Great Britain and, above all, in Germany; in France it dropped sharply. France then became a country with few children and remained so until the middle of our century.

This phenomenon, so important to the history of France, cannot be examined in detail; we shall only touch upon a few essential aspects. Until the end of the nineteenth century the increase in longevity was great enough to hide the consequences of the sharp drop in the birth rate. When the French fully realized what was happening, it was too late to react. It will take almost as many generations to recreate a psychology favorable to a higher birth rate as elapsed between the time that births started dropping and the time the nation understood the meaning of the decline.

A further consequence during the second half of the nineteenth century is that France did not participate in the great emigration movement that prevailed among western European nations. England, Germany, and Russia contributed significantly to the great peopling of the world by the white race. But during the same period France became a country of immigration.

Statistics and simple reflection bring out with clarity the relatively weak economic and political situation of France since the middle of the nineteenth century compared with that of Great Britain, Germany, or even Italy. She was "relatively weak" because her population was rising far more slowly than that of her neighbors. A contrast was established between what seemed like a predominantly static nation and dynamic peoples. The contrast stood out all the more sharply since the factor of longevity played a greater role than the birth factor and thus the average age of the French population was rising.

We have already mentioned the cycle of generations with low birth rates. Every twenty years a small or "hollow" generation procreated another "hollow" generation. This cycle, belonging to the over-all trend toward an aging population, aggravated, from generation to generation, the deficiencies created by the "hollow" periods.

This biological rhythm, so unfavorable to France, can be offered as one of the fundamental causes of her misfortunes from 1870 to 1939. The resultant impression of weakness that France gave between 1910 and 1914 may also have been one of the causes of the First World War. The comparatively innocuous character of the 1890 crisis was due in part to a massive influx of immigrants which brought the nation a measure of youthfulness for the next thirty years.

If there was a wave of immigration toward France in 1880–1900, it was undoubtedly because the French demographic situation had created a zone of attraction in the very heart of an overpopulated Europe. It was also because French economic activity lent itself to the massive assimilation of young foreigners in their most productive years.

We must insist on a capital factor. Starting in 1870 or 1875, the French economy ran on a profit, practically for the first time since the beginning of the technical era.

Let us look again at the maps of French industry in 1780, 1880, and 1930 (Figures 3–5). French industries were not definitively established until after 1880. The initiatives taken during the years 1870–1880 were, at long last, the sound ones. We should also mention the relatively early (by 1830) and happy location of industry in Alsace. It was an auspicious move, but, alas, it was Germany who profited by it when it occupied Alsace in 1871. The withdrawal of many Alsatian factories into the Vosges district in 1871 was a noble and patriotic gesture, but not an economic one, for it is at the origin of the economic crisis afflicting that region today. Generally, the efforts of the nineteenth century to induce technical progress in regions which had been industrial at a much earlier time ended in failures and deep disappointment.

This discouragement appears to be one of the causes of French Malthusianism. We shall insist on this point.

The Malthusian theory is English. We know how widespread have been the propaganda for and the teaching of birth control in England, and how facilities to help its practical application have multiplied. In France there is nothing of the sort. And yet birth control has been much more effective in France than in England. French thought and propaganda have been firmly anti-Malthusian. For once French practice and not French theory is at fault.

The fact is that in Britain and Germany the rapid and secure success of industrialization inspired powerful forces of hope in the psychology of the masses. When France's neighbors undertake a business, no matter how mediocre it really is, they succeed. If in those countries legislation ruling commercial failures was pitilessly applied, it was because failures were relatively rare by comparison with the great number of successes. In France the tendency was quite different. In spite of the constant solicitude of the state and of extreme care in investments, the first industrial ventures were not successes; they only took root after a veritable cascade of failures (except in southern Alsace). The French South and West failed as great textile centers, while Berry and Champagne lost their position as metallurgical centers. In like fashion the first French railways collapsed disastrously, creating that prodigious credit crisis which, despite poor crops, brought prices tumbling down in 1847 and paved the way for the Revolution of 1848. The role of Napoleon III, who considered himself a disciple of Saint-Simon, consisted in strongly encouraging the concentration of industries, just as the old monarchy had influenced industrial concentration in Anzin and Le Creusot. Though relatively concentrated, French industry seemed very precarious until 1870. After that date a new phase of technical transformation took place: electricity, chemistry, and aluminum favored locations which had been rejected until then. The new steel industry gave increased value to the Lorraine deposits. This explains the industrial surge and the call to immigrants which extended the period of French reawakening to the end of the First World War.

In any event, until 1870 Malthusianism was theoretical in England, practical and effective in France, in both demography and economics. This picture corroborates Sismondi's cry, "Close the laboratories, suspend technical progress." French industrial failures were particularly irritating since France was perfectly aware of her scientific and technical superiority. The very difficulties which faced French industry forced her to discover new processes and train the finest technicians. Blast furnaces and cokeries had been recovering their chemical by-products in France long before England realized it could be profitable to do so. But, what is merely an additional profit to the British was a dramatic need to the French—a necessary effort, but not a sufficient one. How readily one understands the exasperation of French engineers in their northern mines, galled by the sight of the rudimentary equipment required to exploit British mines and by the small amount of capital that the English immobilized in order to consolidate and ventilate their shafts. As a matter of fact, nature is less hostile, more generous, in England than in France. France is *obliged* to do outright what England can choose to put off until she feels moved to do so.

Sensitive to injustice, France reacted to the injustice of her geographical lot by practicing Malthusianism. Brilliantly lucid in technical matters, it is in the name of principles that France ridicules Anglo-German Malthusian propaganda: "To lower oneself to such base considerations, what ludicrous vulgarity!" Yet, truly discouraged, she practiced the Malthusianism which she condemned. No need for France to print brochures, to organize lectures, or to teach Malthusian practices. A lack of faith in industry and technical progress was enough to spread rapidly the practice of Malthusianism in the French urban population.

In the countryside the situation was not at all the same. While the industrial and urban population was Malthusian from 1800 on, the rural elements remained prolific until 1840 or thereabouts (see Figure 1). The exodus from country to city (the result not of urban attraction, but of rural discouragement) increased the Malthusian portion of the population. Bound by tradition the rural areas retained a fairly high birth rate until 1875. Rural technique was progressing at that time, though not on the same revolutionary scale as it was in Great Britain and Germany. Even in the 1950's the basic agrarian structures remain what they were in the eighteenth century, for all progress comes from the city, and French cities do not have enough faith in progress to communicate it to the countryside.

Again we face a strange contrast. In a peremptory manner, starting with the eighteenth century, English elites and parliamentary majorities imposed upon the agrarian areas reforms of structure which completely upset the old rural social classes and eliminated small landholders. The same change occurred in Germany. In France informed opinion and governments were far more reticent. How could they ever impose upon the farm districts reforms which had been but semisuccesses in the urban centers? In the French rural areas, then, the population remained faithful to the tradition of large families while practicing an economic Malthusianism of the same general type as that prevailing in the cities. It is a commonplace in French political doctrine to present rural traditionalism as a guarantee of stability. In the middle of the twentieth century Pétain, a Marshal of France, could still evoke the worn-out cliché of the farmer and the artisan as saviors of France without provoking the laughter of public opinion —in fact, only a few voices rose in protest.

A further misfortune was added to the preceding ones. In the 1880's, when French industry was at last registering a few encouraging results, immense shipments of North and South American agricultural products poured into France. It was a disaster for the farmer. As a result Méline (protectionist and Prime Minister from 1896 to 1898) attacked the economic liberalism which for the last fifteen or twenty years had been giving new life to French industry and achieving its necessary concentration. To defend her backward farms France built tariff barriers, which succeeded in protecting economic Malthusianism but failed to protect farm districts from demographic Malthusianism. The shock of 1880 was severe; it aggravated several internal crises (notably in the wine regions). In turn, the birth rate of agrarian France dropped at an accelerated rate.

All of France is not Malthusian; but everywhere, in every domain of activity, the Malthusian party, without ever so calling itself, has taken the upper hand and proved that French psychology doubted, and after one hundred trying years has continued to doubt, the validity of urban and rural technical progress. Certain privileged urban and rural regions barely managed to escape the Malthusian trend: Flanders, Alsace, Brittany. Southwestern France, where agriculture was the most prosperous before becoming the most threatened, where industry was weakest, became the chosen land of Malthusianism.

This is then the picture—an all-conquering theory offset by Malthusianism. The deep break between thought and action is the foundation of the French mind: intelligent, critical, skeptical, full of fire and ardor in the realm of theoretical expression, full of caution and of ironic skepticism is practical economic and social fields.

Any authentic economic success awakens suspicion in France. Everyone immediately wonders, "How could he succeed where so many failed? He must have obtained illicit favors from the state." The dynamic businessman, who announces ambitious projects and fails, is sure to be greeted with a certain smile, or even with affectionate laughter; for everyone will consider his failure part of a common destiny and the instinctive reaction of most Frenchmen will be to come to his help in order that something at least may be saved from disaster.

The same attitude prevails in many countries of South America where nature is harder yet, where the earth, and particularly the subsoil, hold cruel disappointments in store. There we can observe the same amused mockery, the same cordiality, the same eloquent pride, the same jeering skepticism. Parisian wit, French wit, is immediately understood in South America; French literature reigns there almost as a national literature.

The French view of life is scarcely understood by the Anglo-Saxon or the German, by people who own abundant supplies of "easy" coal. The French view of life is a Latin one: the Mediterranean has no coal.

These facts should not be interpreted as proof that France has no outstanding technical, industrial, or rural achievements to her credit. The obstacles France encountered are at the origin of an undeniable superiority in the theoretical realm. French industrial models and mechanical prototypes are incomparable. And at times, through sheer effort—on the state's part, that is—France arrives at obvious practical successes: her nationalized railroads, her nationalized coal mines, have always been models for the world to follow. Though less frequent, the efforts of individual groups have been crowned with success in the rare occurrences where nature showed herself bountiful: metallurgy thriving on iron ore, chemical industries on soft coal, aluminum on bauxite with nearby electric power, and so forth. But in every instance one realized what a cleavage separates the efficient minority blessed by nature from an ill-favored, grumbling, skeptical, and Malthusian majority. This majority demands that superhighways be free (tolls are levied in Anglo-Saxon countries and even in Italy) and that railroads lower their rates to the point of running on a permanent deficit.

In Anglo-Saxon countries efficiency is a virtue. In France the popular notion of justice rises against so categorical a view. Efficiency is rather taken to be the sign of a privileged individual accountable for his successes to the collectivity and obliged to pay heavy tribute to the community in compensation for his exceptional luck. In France virtue is more naturally associated with misfortune and calamity, with the wisdom of those who refuse to sacrifice the relative satisfactions of today to the uncertain successes of tomorrow.

Every Frenchman experiences the nostalgic attraction of luxury. A very modest sort of luxury, to be sure, since the majority of the population is poor. The luxuries of the home—modern comfort, running water, municipal sewage, and the like—are costly items requiring faith in the future and the payment of high rentals to a landlord who, as a privileged individual, is the instinctive object of deep-rooted suspicion. As a consequence, Frenchmen are resigned to poor housing and voiced indignation when, in the 1920's, Germany proved more interested in building bathrooms for workmen than in settling war reparations.

But the story is a different one for the luxuries the Frenchman can afford; he uses and abuses them, as in the case of wine. The history of wine in France is a surprising one. First of all let us discard that old cliché according to which alcoholism is a disaster for which our immoral modern cities are responsible. In reality, technically progressive cities are, the world over, the lowest consumers of wine. The tender spot France has for wine and its substitutes is of rural origin. As the result of hard, intelligent labor and, in this instance, nature's favor, French vineyards were a subject of universal admiration in the eighteenth century. Arthur Young, not very indulgent toward France, recognized the fact. Many forward steps in European agriculture stemmed from the lucid observations of French winegrowers. Thus, as far back as the eighteenth century the whole French people enjoyed the privilege of being wine consumers. Since that time the protection of winegrowers has always been considered a national duty. The best assurance of economic protection being the mass consumption of wine, the habit became almost a virtue. We shall see through what stages this came about.

Until 1814 wine was relatively more expensive than wheat. From 1814 to 1850 its price dropped; consumption rose. From 1850 to 1900 the price rose again, but the habit had been acquired; there was no drop in consumption. The price had risen because grape parasites had destroyed crops and created underproduction; wine had to be imported. The world's greatest wine producer also became its greatest importer. Furthermore, in the 1850's the appearance of the *oïdium,* a severe grape mildew, resulted in a greater production of beet alcohol, which partially replaced wine in the public's taste. There again the acquired habit did not disappear. However, when wine production resumed its normal output, the prices did not drop to the earlier level: by a typically French reaction the nation assumed that it was a major duty of hers to protect the winegrowers, deserving fellows whom ingrate nature had so meanly treated! Winegrowing then became an exceedingly profitable business. It expanded immoderately from a production of 154 million gallons in the eighteenth to one of 330 millions in the middle of our century. Most of it is now consumed by the cities; more clever, the farmers only drink what they cannot sell. For the average Frenchman, to drink wine is both a necessary luxury and a patriotic duty. Toward 1900 he was told that wine would bring social peace. In 1910 it was described as the health of the strong and the strength of the weak. In 1919 it was heralded as a major cause of victory in the late war. It was called upon to save the franc in 1922.

France accomplished a miracle: she established in Algeria, in the midst of a Moslem civilization, some of the world's most splendid vineyards. Today she is paying the consequences of this dangerous miracle.

Winegrowing is the most profitable and the most secure branch of French agriculture. If only France applied to all of her industries the fixed policy of her winegrowers: first sell, then consume! But winegrowers find an easy domestic market and they insist on monopolizing it. For this reason they were ready by 1922 to come to some sort of agreement with their archrivals, the beet alcohol manufacturers.

We shall not treat here the distressing subject of the scandalous subsidies granted to producers of beet alcohol. The more one enters into the details of the problem, the more one despairs of ever arriving at a solution profitable to the nation rather than to the distillers. Yet the distillers with their bountiful lands and their enormous profits have none of the historical arguments used by the winegrowers.

There exists in France an undeniable attraction for luxury, for a modest sort of luxury, perhaps the most elementary of all, but carried to an extreme degree of perfection—the luxury of fine eating. The history of wine is paralleled by that of beefsteak.

In addition to the gastronomic luxuries, there is luxury in dress. This applies particularly to women. (Frenchmen seem to adore women all the more when they expect no children from them. Is this a way of making amends?) During the nineteenth century women played a more discreet role in France than in Great Britain, Germany, or, above all, the United States where they tend to become the stronger sex. Nevertheless, they significantly contributed in the orientation of French production toward luxury.

One cannot accuse French women of having imposed the trend toward luxury characteristic of the national production. They only drew the best possible advantage from what was an economic necessity. This deserves explanation.

When one reads the frequently justified complaints uttered by French industrialists in the 1830's, one meets with the following statement: French textile fabrics, because handmade, are of the highest quality, infinitely superior to the machine-made British fabrics. In 1890 the French denounced German "junk." Doubtless, French fabrics, spun on small looms, were perfectly adapted to changing fashions, to original designs made in very limited yardage and intended to be quickly replaced. The Anglo-German machinery was decidedly less versatile; it produced cheap materials in mass quantities.

During all of the nineteenth century the world's aristocracy exhibited a marked preference for French luxury fabrics, particularly, silks and woolens. It was fashionable for Londoners to dress in Paris, even for men (it was probably a sort of inferiority complex which inspired French males to affect a preference for English styles and fabrics; Frenchwomen were not so naïve). In the same way the famous *articles de Paris* (trinkets, garments, etchings, perfumes, accessories; delicate gifts of all sorts) were quite the furor. In this line the French were unmatched—even by the Viennese, who did their best to follow the French example prompted, as they were, by an equally hard struggle against physical handicaps unfavorable to modern industrialization. Now to make as much money as possible at the expense of foreigners, thanks to the renowned originality of the French artisan, requires great skill in varying the whims of fashion—not so much variety that the "luxury" clientele will be discouraged, yet enough to wage an endless war of nerves with powerful foreign industrialists. A sense of elegance, the proverbial taste of her people and particularly of her women, has always been one of the great assets of France's economy.

However, there should have arisen no abuse of the situation, no tendency to become the victim of one's own game. In truth, the women of France were cleverer than the men. Of all branches of the luxury industry, that devoted to women proved the most durable, the most sensible—at least in the nineteenth century. Today the ingenious creations of French women have lost some of their universal prestige. The luxury clientele now comprises but a small elite. Today the famed silk trade of Lyons relies greatly on church orders for survival, and the advent of nylon almost wiped out French superiority.

Sooner or later France will have to recognize that the 1830 motto, "Quality can only be hand made," is out of date.

France sought consolation for inferiority in the realm of agricultural and industrial mass production in the superiority enjoyed by her luxury trade.

The genial instinct toward luxury accommodated itself too well with demographic Malthusianism not to sustain it, encourage it, and finally prejudice industrial progress. The objective should have been the discovery of a palliative to the difficulties facing French industry, not the abandonment of industrialization. Everything that gives an absolute, definitive character to the praise of wine, food, fashion, and luxury transforms what could have been a hope of remedy into a distressing vice. It creates a grave error of appreciation as to the direction of humanity's evolution toward the basic well-being of the great possible number of men, not toward a few exquisite experiences.

"The superfluous, such a very necessary thing!" sang Voltaire, the courtier of His New Majesty the Bourgeois, in a century when courtiers revolved around the Absolute Monarch. Perhaps Voltaire really was a century ahead. But truly, does not his saying sound hopelessly out of place in the middle of the twentieth century?

V

Adventurous Courage

FRANCE is a military nation. The ease with which her absolute monarchy recruited troops, long esteemed the world's finest, was envied by neighboring rulers. From the eighteenth century on, France surpassed the rest of Europe in her military spirit. One might have supposed that this was a distinctly monarchical trait and that the love of glory and honor which Montesquieu and Vauvenargues attributed to France would have given place to new virtues in the face of the technical progress that fostered the great political transformations at the end of the eighteenth century. On the contrary, France was more passionately military after the Revolution than before.

We have noted how technical progress in France encountered innumerable physical obstacles. These very difficulties kept alive France's military vocation. Or at least, the history of the Revolution leads one to this belief.

At its inception the Constituent Assembly did not have in mind the slightest military adventure. Its sole concern was to establish a constitutional and juridical system that would open vast horizons to technical progress and encourage the expansion of legitimate middle-class ambitions

—more specifically, the ambitions of the bourgeois from the Gironde, the Loire, the Rhone, and the Seine. But from the outset it appeared that this pacific constitutional revolution was impossible without the support of the Paris masses. And so the bourgeois who made up the membership of the Constituent Assembly were obliged to accept the unexpected and, at times, the downright embarrassing support of Paris. The first blows dealt to the old corporative, state-ruled social structure threw artisans and laborers of every sort out of their secular framework. By a sudden conversion brewers, butchers, cobblers, became armed chieftains excited by the summer sun. And in a matter of months practically every French town followed suit.

Any break in France's ever-fragile economic setup provokes a phenomenon of the same order. The old monarchy had experienced it more than once. The phenomenon is not peculiar to France. England and Germany underwent it, notably in the seventeenth century. Still, in the 1790's the English situation was vastly different from that of France. Across the Channel the population, barely freed of the old rural framework, was in good part caught up and integrated into the new industrial and urban activity. The Luddites, the notorious machine breakers, were relatively weak; the "forces of law and order" were able to dominate them.

In France the situation soon revealed itself to be profoundly disturbing. In the spring of 1789 the anxious Court called to the army for help. The populace of Paris then took to arms. The victory of the Parisians increased the anxiety of courtiers, who began emigrating. The subsequent halt in luxury industries brought with it an immediate reduction of economic activity: far from pressing forward, urban development receded. Hence a new mass of unemployed. The trend amplified, the Court disappeared, and the urban population fell into a sort of permanent state of mobilization. Though less extensive the general tendency was the same in the farmlands—particularly in the most progressive areas.

And so the liberal Assemblies of the Revolution were confronted with the most unexpected consequences. Made up of bourgeois, they had hoped to give the nation a progressive, liberal, and technical organization on the British pattern. Tearing down the old economic structures, they unwittingly conjured up an immense popular army, which organized itself into sections, elected leaders, and seized and manufactured arms. Steadily increasing, the army was a constant threat. In a state of permanent mobilization, it first moved against the king's troops. Citizens from Paris and Marseilles fought the king's Swiss Guards on August 10, 1792. Then, as a natural consequence the new army deployed over Europe. The success of the recruitment drive was due much less to the burning eloquence of Danton than to the availability of masses of chronic unemployed. Jurists and theoreticians had simply not foreseen the curious offspring of their brilliant proclamations. And it was absolutely in vain that they attempted two or three times (notably, during the riots in the Champ-de-Mars) to integrate the spontaneous popular army within the economic order. After their failure the peaceful jurists themselves were struck by delirium and preached war with feverish ardor. A patriot was then understood to be a man who was both a sincere revolutionary and an authentic soldier fighting on the nation's frontiers.

The revolutionary extremists, conscious of a movement that was going to deplete the great cities of their revolutionary troops by sending them to the frontier battlefields, resolved to crush any possibility of a future counterrevolutionary insurrection—hence the terrible massacres of September 1792.

By 1793 France was a single great army. One must read the proclamations of the National Convention and those of the Committees of Public Safety to realize the scope of a psychological mobilization that included women, children, and old people. Everyone worked for the army. What about British liberalism? It had gone with the winds of war. The moderate Girondist deputies were sent to the guillotine. The extremists of the Mountain Party took over dictatorial powers. Total war was being waged on two fronts: against foreign troops and against internal enemies, for the poor rural areas (particularly in the West), which had remained somewhat outside the spontaneous mobilization of the first years, did not accept conscription and preferred to fight their own war at home, in the Vendée, against the Revolution.

The dictatorship by the Mountain Party was that of a people in arms—a technocratic and military dictatorship which brought to the fore technicians and generals of very great talent, such as Gaspard Monge and Lazare Carnot. Victory followed.

It was a common saying then that victories hounded Robespierre like a pack of furies. In effect, victories tend to inflame leaders. Could the Republic have turned an immense army living off war to peaceful economic activities? If so, it would have achieved the world's most spectacular reconversion. Unfortunately, the physical obstacles were too great for the rapid industrialization of a country cut off by the British navy from normal trading in the Atlantic. And little by little, the civil power degenerated;

only one element, the army, retained its pristine strength. Bonaparte imposed himself despite his political mediocrity —a mediocrity brilliantly, if reticently, shown by Guglielmo Ferrero.

Bonaparte, the First Consul, was acclaimed because he was expected to bring peace. But he was no more capable than Barras of developing industry sufficiently to absorb the manpower of a nation under arms. And so that enormous army kept marching back and forth from Boulogne to Moscow, from Amsterdam to Naples and Cadiz—always cut off from the seas which could have borne the great trade needed to regenerate French economic activity (Mollien had counted on this at the time of the Peace of Amiens).

After 1815 France deliberately placed herself in England's wake. She developed a commercial fleet and undertook a vast plan of industrialization. Decazes, a prominent minister, founded the mining town that bears his name. Parliamentarianism became serious business. The masses, however, were waiting, regretting the past, criticizing, hoping, and stirring impatiently; they still dreamed of military glory. The conquest of Algeria occurred too late; it was not the real initiators of the campaign, the Bourbons, but Louis Philippe who profited by it. The government of Charles X had already surmised that the conquest of Algeria might "open the door to emigrations both necessary to the domestic tranquillity of France and useful to her grandeur," but the government of Louis Philippe realized this program. As early as 1831 the Paris police prefect enrolled thousands of Parisians, who, as Baude wrote, "had been placed at the permanent disposal of social agitators by hard times," and sent them away as volunteer settlers in Algeria. Above all, the Algerian war offered a way out to a great number of Frenchmen hungering for adventure and glory; in fact, 100,000 found death. So long as the Algerian campaign lasted, the government of Louis Philippe enjoyed domestic peace. Once it ended, Paris resumed its agitation.

Exactly what did Baude mean by "hard times"? He was referring to the industrial mobilization tearing farmhands away from their hovels and artisans away from their shops. If industrial employment was strong, all went well. If not, riots and street fighting rapidly broke out. The old revolutionary and military blood, the old patriotic temperament, would boil anew; and woe to the throne! In 1840 the French railroads tore workers away from their old routines to hire them as construction laborers. In the financial crisis of 1847 many of the laborers lost their jobs. The following year Paris was in arms, and the street fighting of June 1848 took on the aspect of a civil war. In 1871 the war with Germany was concluded—and poorly so, at that—but thereupon Thiers, a narrow champion of capitalism, was confronted with a terrible civil war which he was incapable of preventing. The National Assembly, being of a Girondist frame of mind, evacuated Paris to sit in Bordeaux, and Thiers crushed the opposition by brutal force.

In 1848 Lamartine was entirely justified in stating that Algiers lay between Paris and the Rhone. It also lay between Paris and the Versailles government of 1871. In other words, colonial expansion was a guarantee of political stability for nineteenth-century France.

Colonial expansion was not restricted to the nineteenth century. France had tried her hand in India and America before succeeding in Africa. Still, the procedure was identical each time; the settlements overseas were established in a radically different manner by France and by England. In England the first emigrants were generally from the wealthier classes; they comprised technicians, people with a modern bent; the poor classes followed. British emigration brought laborers over only after capital and capital equipment had arrived. Scarcely ashore, British emigrants built ships and towns, establishing solid and permanent contacts between the new lands and the old country. English cities in India or in America grew at a record speed. And the coastal activity of these industrial ports and cities was intense enough to delay the conquest of the hinterland. The attraction, for the British, was definitely along the sea.

From the eighteenth century on the men who came to France were technicians, German mining engineers, and bankers, notably Swiss bankers. But those who left France were simple folk, peasants, unskilled laborers. In France's colonies capital and technicians were scarce. Among the emigrants were few artisans and few tools. Report after report was sent from Quebec to Versailles to deplore the complete lack of artisans, carpenters, and wheelwrights. The French settlers scattered; they built little villages only. They had few ships, not much commerce. The Frenchman had to renounce his native land, to throw himself into the adventurous conquest of a new continent. He started out on foot. A poor builder of cities, he excelled in the discovery and exploration of the hinterland. Incapable of interesting European merchants and financiers in his venture, he interested himself in native inhabitants attracted by his vocation for discovery and farming. The Frenchmen who lived in India and the Frenchmen who settled in American did not restrict themselves to the seashores, where rather sickly little military villages had been erected; they marched deep into the continents, melting into the immense new lands. Such also is the history of French Africa.

THE FRENCH AND THE REPUBLIC

When English maritime settlements consolidated, they would seize French villages, cutting off the interior French possessions from their homeland. It was a child's game, assuredly—an Englishman's game—after that to integrate the small French colonist into London's vast economic network. Such was France's fate in India and in America (see Figure 6).

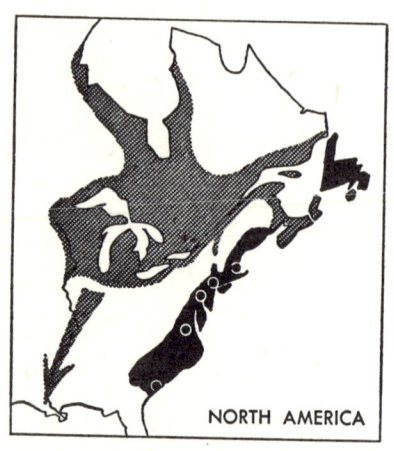

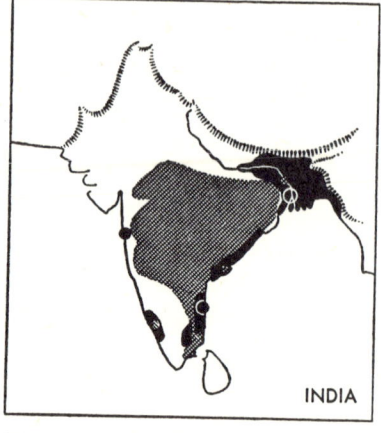

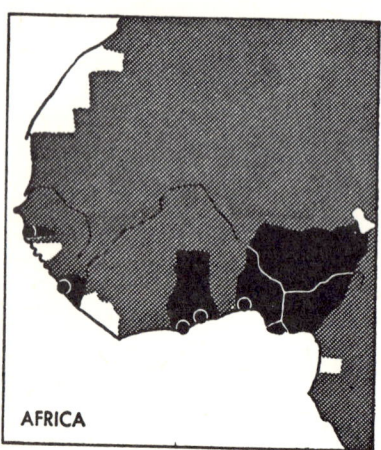

FIGURE 6. The French (*gray*) and the English (*black*) in North America (17th Century), India (18th Century), and Africa (19th Century).

The same adventure was repeated three times. In the seventeenth century the French scattered into the American interior. In 1753 Dupleix held the interior of India (where the English were never to gain a firm hold). In 1900 the French were masters of the heart of dark Africa. The Frenchman is bound to the earth. The Englishman hugs the coasts, where he builds ports and keeps in contact with his homeland.

In Algeria, however, the Marseilles-Algiers crossing was short enough for the North African frontier to behave as an urban prolongation of southern France. That is why North Africa escaped the natural destiny of French possessions. But then, what astonishing success! No nation in the nineteenth century can boast of a colonization comparable to that of Algeria.

In South Africa, in Australia, the problems of settling were elementary beside the innumerable geographical and ethnical difficulties which the French surmounted in Algeria. Someday, we hope, the great, the fascinating, history of Algeria will be written.

And what of Indochina? It is an exception to the rule; it was purely a naval expedition. Consequently, the colonization of Indochina more or less followed the British pattern of trading and industrialization. Nevertheless, in Indochina also, though on a smaller scale, earthbound French settlers rooted themselves more deeply, in more intimate contact with the indigenous population, than did the British in India. It was on too small a scale, however, for the settling to be permanent. As a matter of fact, the colonization of Indochina survived that of India by only a few years. But the conclusion of the Indochinese affair differs markedly from the conclusion of England's occupation of India. In India, England, ever a shrewd tradesman, observed that the occupation ledger was showing an increasing deficit, and she resolved to close a business once prosperous but now threatened by bankruptcy. In Indochina the stubborn French, more deeply rooted to the soil, preferred to wage war. This character trait has been repeatedly demonstrated in French history over the last ten centuries. At the time of the Crusades, while Frederick Hohenstaufen and the Republic of Venice were negotiating and trading with the Infidels, France's holy kings dreamed only of glorious battles in Palestine.

This brings us back to our main theme: patriotic war against all forms of coalition forces, street fighting against the police forces of monarchical or parliamentary regimes, and the successful conquest of the soil by colonial settlers. All three traits reveal the same basic character element, adventurous courage. All three reveal the same economic feature, hesitation to develop commerce and industry.

Truly, Napoleon III may have been sincere when he proclaimed: "The Empire means Peace." Author of *Extinction du paupérisme,* a stanch follower of Saint-Simon, and a man knowing England intimately, he was justified in believing that all of France's energy would be absorbed by the gigantic accomplishments he dreamed of giving her: railroads, canals, salvaging of deserted land, urban planning, modernization of the steel and textile industries to allow competition with Great Britain, freedom of international trade capable of converting Bordeaux, Rouen, or Paris into Bristols and Londons. After all Napoleon I had had the same dream for several months.

At that Napoleon III was more successful in this domain than his illustrious uncle, thanks to the progress realized by the parliamentary monarchies. But he did not go far enough. Energetic as the French industrial effort may have been, a large fraction of the population remained unaffected by it. As a consequence, our dreamy-eyed disciple of Saint-Simon was obliged once more to ride painfully the old war horse. The campaigns of Crimea and Italy ensued. Again the Empire meant war—but a war lacking inner convictions, a dilettante's war. The fatal shock with Bismarck was inevitable.

The war waged by the French was quite different from

the Germans'. In 1830 the technical structure of Germany was roughly comparable to that of France about 1750. In 1880 the German technical structure had reached a level that England was not to approximate until 1900. Such an explosion could not occur without violently tearing the people from their rural settings and placing them at the permanent disposal of the army. Such an industrial explosion encourages, above all, armaments and an organization of a highly technical nature. The Frenchman resigns himself to the fact of war, then wages it with earthly qualities of endurance, faith, and abnegation which make him one of the world's remarkable soldiers. Yet fundamentally he makes war because he cannot make industries; hence his armament is deficient. Germany wages war, carried forward by an industrial whirlwind which gives it steel and a systematically planned mobilization. Clearly this seems to be the lesson of 1871.

One should add, out of regard for the obvious qualities of French theoretical technicians, that, if France did not have the same industrially produced firearms which Germany had, yet by 1870 she owned the world's finest prototypes, but in such limited numbers as to be practically useless.

We have mentioned the powerful surge of industrialization which inspired the parliamentary and republican France of 1890.

France from 1876 to 1885 welcomed numerous foreigners—urban workman, masons, and plasterers from Spain and Italy as well as Jews of small and great fortunes. The anti-Semitic Edouard Drumont and the xenophobes waxed furious, echoing those who, after Jean Baptiste Say, had bitterly reproached French colonial emigration for draining the nation of its vital substance. Nevertheless, through these measures the French population was rejuvenated and re-equipped.

In 1914, consequently, France was better armed than in 1870. There then emerged the sturdy peasantlike qualities of the French soldier for whom the mud of the trenches became a symbol of national reconciliation. Heroism, blood, glory, deaths. But 1918 was too beautiful a victory!

French industry came out of the war badly. The nation soon had to give up any hope of meaningful war reparations. Once again German industrial superiority had armed and organized Germany with such foresight that the war had been waged on French soil. In 1919 German industrial potential was left intact. Whereupon the Anglo-Saxon world, lost in admiration of the achievements of German technique, was quick to assist in the further expansion of German industry.

In 1940 Hitler was right in stating that French cannons were made of straw. Once more, in spite of having the world's finest engineers, the French bared their chests to the machinery pouring out of the powerful German factories. And once more France could boast of owning superior prototypes in nearly every military field.

The road of retreat that led from Tours to Bordeaux, and from Bordeaux to Vichy, crossed the nonindustrial zones of France. Along that sad road were found the mottoes that would rule Vichy's National Revolution, which at best was a sorry return to the eighteenth century: glorification of peasant and artisan, regionalism, turnip planting, and city vegetable gardens! The French were hurt at realizing that their industry had again failed them. Faced by a German production that only Britain could match, they returned to the soil.

But to fight with wooden staves against steel weapons, to tear out cobblestones and block streets, to cheat the police, in short, to resist, came naturally. A century and a half had prepared the French for the Resistance movement. Likewise, the fact of being liked and respected by native populations through four centuries of successful experience was to make of French Africa the springboard of Allied victory.

Adventurous courage? It is born of what the Italians call the *furia francese,* the French fury, the battle ardor of the French. It is the fury of a people that during the rural centuries was the greatest Western nation, a fury that has never abated since France's rivals turned the arms of industry against her—an industry which France rebuilds untiringly, which nature untiringly betrays, and which the enemy lays waste; an industry which her best friends help rebuild but with a thrifty eye to their own interests.

But let these cautious friends take heed. France requires a war industry by necessity, not by taste. Today she is closely observing the methods by which the great rural peoples of Asia, the Russians and the Chinese, have organized their industrial successes. The *furia francese,* if defeated in the Ardennes, in Indochina, in Africa, might look for its age-old recourse, revolution. Would it make a clean sweep of unlucky capitalism and unlucky parliamentarianism? Would it put proletarian techniques to good use? Would such a revolution finally give France an industrial might worthy of her past rural power? This is hardly the place to consider these questions.

And it matters little if anger should one day seize the people of 1789, 1830, 1848, 1871, 1914, and 1944. Whether that revolution is the last spasm of a discouraged nation or the start of a new age, you may be sure it will be brutal, and it will take the non-French world completely by surprise.

VI

Political Insecurity

LET us recapitulate the characteristics of contemporary France: a passion for theory (both in terms of a juridical exigency and in the aspiration toward scientific and technical eminence), economic anxiety, Malthusianism, an inclination toward luxury, adventurous courage. How could such discordant elements be expected to engender a coherent political thought or a stable regime?

The juridical exigency carries with it a curious sequel: French constitutional evolution is not supple and gradual as it is in Great Britain. It rests on rigid texts modifiable, to be sure, but not without resorting to complex ceremonials and procedures. The lengthiness of the procedures ruling consitutional changes is frequently the cause of popular outbursts and of extralegal political measures. Ultimately, constitutional changes become the objectives of revolutions and *coups d'état*: 1789, 1793, 1799, 1815, 1830, 1848, 1851, 1871, 1940, 1944.

Since England has no written constitution, it is impossible to define with precision the boundaries of her constitutional life. In particular, one may wonder whether her two-party system is an integral part of the governmental organization or not. Pragmatism would imply an affirmative answer. But France has never dared mention the organization of parties in her many constitutions. The danger inherent in written constitutions rests in the blanks they leave in the margins of the texts. It is true that parties are not written into the American constitution either. But is that certain? Isn't the American constitution really inspired by two great poles of attraction: the tendency toward reinforcing the federal government and the tendency toward reinforcing state and local government? This double theme of individual freedom or of collective union permeates the constitutional and political history of the United States. France, on the contrary, very rapidly subordinated local powers to the central government and limited the autonomy of the *départements* by forcing them into a rigid administrative framework. With it all, France never concerns herself about the life of parties. Even in the heat of the Revolution, the famous Jacobins' Club, a *de facto* institution, was not an institution by constitutional rights.

The organic character of British parties is self evident. For two centuries they organized and asserted themselves. They were schools where political leaders were slowly trained. Parties cast their eyes upon the most brilliant university students in order to turn them quite early to political life. For this reason there exists in England a coherent political society distributed along two axes. Great Britain has experienced the distressing crises of multiparty politics: in the 1890's there were no less than four parties as a result of dissatisfaction on the extreme right and the extreme left. But such splits were quickly healed, and so it was that the Liberal Party gave way to the Labor Party.

French constitutional theories have been so widely copied that their narrow definition of the constitutional domain today seems natural. The notion of this limitation stems from the theoretical presumption that one can delimit what is constitutional from what is not. That very notion inspired Bentham's most beautiful pages of parliamentary sophistry. Appropriately, it was this Anglo-Saxon who gave France a lesson that she chose to ignore. And the French point of view so perfectly suited the multiparty systems which dominated continental Europe that even Russian thought hesitated before the problem of making specific constitutional provisions in favor of the Communist Party—this, in spite of incontestable organic unity.

One must bear in mind that the very existence of parties was profoundly repulsive to the French monarchy, implying, as it did, the idea of civil war. Strangely enough the Republic inherited this repulsion. French constitutions exclude regulation of party organization; this originates in a feeling handed down from the Old Regime rather than in any analysis of the British scene.

Both juridical rigidity and the multiparty system derive from the fact that a notable portion of French public opinion at once refuses technical progress on the bourgeois English pattern and its political corollary, parliamentarianism. For this reason, the existence of two great parties is impossible. The French regime fosters at least five types of parties. Once fragmentation sets in, there is no way to stop it.

Obviously, the multiparty structure implies little parties with a weak machine, weak cadres, and uncertain resources—parties incapable of educating public opinion. British parties are as much parliamentary schools for future prime ministers, who serve as active members during

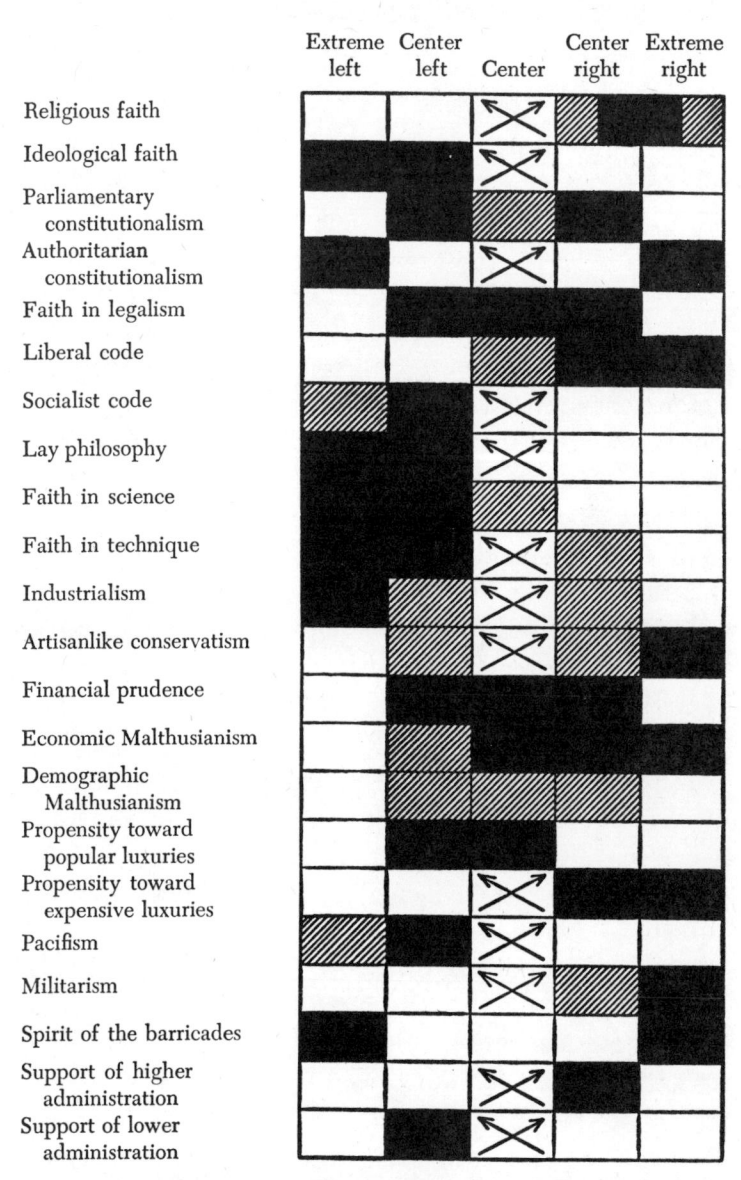

	Extreme left	Center left	Center	Center right	Extreme right
Religious faith			⤫	▨	▨
Ideological faith	■		⤫		
Parliamentary constitutionalism		■	▨		
Authoritarian constitutionalism	■		⤫		■
Faith in legalism		■	■	■	
Liberal code			▨	■	
Socialist code	▨	■	⤫		
Lay philosophy	■	■	⤫		
Faith in science	■	■	▨		
Faith in technique			⤫	▨	
Industrialism	■	▨	⤫	▨	
Artisanlike conservatism		▨	⤫	▨	■
Financial prudence		■	■	■	
Economic Malthusianism		▨	■	■	
Demographic Malthusianism		▨	▨	▨	▨
Propensity toward popular luxuries		■	■		
Propensity toward expensive luxuries			⤫		
Pacifism	▨	■	⤫		
Militarism			⤫	▨	■
Spirit of the barricades	■		■		
Support of higher administration			⤫	■	
Support of lower administration		■	⤫		

FIGURE 7. Dominating Traits of the Five Major French Political Tendencies.

By its very nature the Center is subject to changes of opinion on most essential points. These changes make for the possibility of governmental evolution and may occur either within one of the Center parties or by the replacement of one Center party by another.

twenty or thirty years before coming to power, as they are schools for a mass of electors regularly followed and informed. French parties teach very little to their deputies and even less to their potential prime ministers. They have no significant educational influence on the electorate.

The French parliamentarian learns his profession on the benches of the National Assembly. Ministers and presidents learn their profession while governing—whence the frequently violent contrasts between what they promise before, they realize during, and they propose after elections. Power in France is as much an apprenticeship as an executive function. The National Assembly is as much a practical school as a deliberating body. An electoral system based on single-member constituencies and two ballots does actually foster political concentrations. In no way, however, does it compensate for the absence of informed citizens and political leaders. To ignore the real problems of government is the common lot of electors and deputies.

It follows that no brake is applied to demagogy. Facing an electorate a good third of which is antiparliamentarian, a new candidate falls into the demagogic vein with an ardor all the more convincing because he is both sincerely naïve and consummately uninformed. In this manner antiparliamentarianism promotes antiparliamentarianism. The Communist Party is unsurpassed at this game: naturally antiparliamentarian, it takes great pains to educate its followers and representatives in the art of antiparliamentarianism. Given the political temperament of the French, this is truly the acme of artfulness. The Communist Party takes advantage of institutions built for *citizens* to exasperate the old mentality of *subjects*. Thus, communism resolves one of the oldest and most alarming contradictions peculiar to the French political temperament. And every so-called "moderate" party has tried to do the same.

Economic anxiety, the mother of economic Malthusianism, is at the source of the characteristic reticence of the French toward basic social transformations. This strong tendency is the essential support of *immobilisme*. The opponents of Guizot were already declaring: "What's the use of government? A boundary mark would be enough." And this a full 120 years before Laniel, the most typical heir of Orleanism, came to power. Yet, from Guizot to Laniel, Orleanism has always sustained a prosperous economy. Yes, truly a prosperous economy, but timid through experience, anxious and cautious by temperament, at times downright frightened. Such prudence sharply contrasts with English movement and German enthusiasm.

The taste for luxury—even that modest popular luxury of seeking the pleasures of refined food—is an element of stability, since it rests on rural permanency and not on industrial progress. At the very heart of *immobilisme*, other French characteristics intervene to create a wicked imbalance: whether to the right or to the left, the passion for theory inspires extreme political formulas. For instance, the excessive stand taken on the matter of property. Thiers's book on property, written immediately after the Revolution of 1848, is quite a revelation. What sonorous, hollow oratory accompanies his haughty, blindly theoretical claims! Though more positive, the claims of the first socialists are no less extreme: "Property is theft," proclaims Proudhon. The exceptional gifts of the French for technique and science have provoked among them strong revolts against immobility. On several occasions these gifts have even served the cause of capitalism, pulling it out of its periodic stagnation. But also these same gifts incite many intellectuals systematically to condemn a capitalistic regime which has always been sickly in France and to affiliate themselves with the extreme Left. That some of France's greatest scientists should, in the recent past, have been Socialists, and today Communists, is a normal reaction arising from their faith in progress and their revolt against the torpor of French traditions.

Clearly, adventurous courage is the greatest single threat to political balance. All we need to do is to reflect on the double meaning of "patriot." In the days of Robespierre it was synonymous with "revolutionary." In France patriotism has always been a characteristic which parties to the extreme left are fully justified in claiming as their own—revolutionary patriotism, that is. But also, from the time of Robespierre the patriot has been the man who marches to the frontiers defending a nation in peril of death. And so the patriot belongs also to the flamboyant factions of the nationalistic Right.

In France it is singularly difficult to foresee the relationships between government and people. The former is frequently too cautious, too fearful, too motionless. Under the cover of prudence and wisdom it blindly refuses any significant reform; and the systematic aspect of French constitutional law contributes to its immobility. On the other hand, the masses, if ever so slightly impelled by a crisis, become exalted; ready to explode, they cry out their indignation.

What sort of a crisis goads them? It can very well be an emotional one, born of passion. Such a crisis generally coincides with an economic strain endangering the French propensity toward luxury. This propensity, we must insist, is a very modest one; if unsatisfied, it would entail a possible drop of living standards below the lowest acknowledged norms for decent survival. Without properly being revolutions dictated by misery—these are rarely productive—revolutions in France are often prompted by a threat of misery, perceptible to the people at large in the realization that their modest "table luxury" is in jeopardy.

In short, the French political regime is comparable to a succession of waterfalls. Various elements oblige the ship of state to anchor at a given level, and it is able to do so in periods of relative technical progress. But let it meet a wave of real difficulties, and the cable breaks; the regime shoots the rapids, tumbling down to a new level where it attempts, once more, to seek firm anchorage.

It is quite useless to comment at any length on the differences which distinguish France from a country of continuous evolution such as Great Britain. We shall merely mention a few essential dates.

In 1789 a revolutionary effort was made to replace the absolute monarchy by a regime tending toward parliamentary government. But it gave only mediocre encouragement to technical progress. Consequently, the most illustrious figures associated with scientific progress were driven to political extremes. From Monge, the creator of descriptive geometry, to Legendre, a fellow mathematician, they collaborated with the National Convention; they even served as members of the Committee of Public Safety. This coincided with the first experiment in proletarian dictatorship. The structural deficiencies of the dictatorial regime and the resultant economic deficiencies provoked a return: first, to a republic with parliamentary trappings, then to an absolute monarchy of military inspiration. The effort made to sever European economy from English technical progress having led to the enrichment of Britain, France resigned herself to going back to a monarchical regime founded basically on the English parliamentary model. For several years this time the government was strengthened by marked progress in the textile field. Unfortunately, an international crisis in the cotton industry (1827–1828) brought about, first, a return to monarchical absolutism with Charles X (he rediscovered the road to war and launched the conquest of Algeria), then the Revolution of 1830. This last event abruptly reformed French economic and political structures while solving the textile situation and re-establishing parliamentary procedure according to the English pattern.

Thereupon occurred a new wave of technical progress. On this occasion the readjustment created a paradoxical situation: French gold, which was hesitant to manufacture in France, went to work for Britain. England built its railroads under the kindly eye of Guizot, the Anglophile, while the ambitious Thiers, taking the leadership of the Anglophobes, fired stupid and facile sarcasms at railroads, considering them the futile plaything of the idle rich. The usual reaction, by then a natural event in French politics, happened: Louis Philippe swung back to absolutism, a sudden revolution overthrew him, the whole French banking and railroad structure was capsized in order forcefully to impose upon the nation the necessary new technical equipment.

An enormous effort to attain systematic progress brought the followers of Saint-Simon to power with the assistance of Napoleon III. The railroad crisis successfully dealt with and the stability afforded by the new technical equipment a proven fact, the country returned to a regime of the British parliamentary type.

Alas, energetic as the French disciples of Saint-Simon may have been, their efforts could not cope with the success of German techniques. The terrible clash of 1870–1871 brought the facts to light: the old patriotic warring nation was crushed by the new technical mastery of the Iron Chancellor ("The Iron and Coal Chancellor," as the excellent Clapham so aptly put it). The worldwide economic crisis beginning in 1872–1873 encouraged, as usual, a resurgence of monarchical dreams. The king's return to Paris was being prepared. Nevertheless, the crisis was overcome by the efforts of French capitalism between 1870 and 1880 and thanks to a noteworthy renewal of interest in the colonization of Algeria. Once again France started treading the path of British parliamentary government.

We have too often brought the importance of French technical successes in the 1880's to the reader's attention to elaborate on them again. From that date on the republican and parliamentarian complexion of the French regime was unquestioned. But it was within a framework narrower than the English one, for it excluded parties; the old French cycle was still at work.

The crisis of 1873 was a long-drawn-out affair. In effect it opened a series of crises intimately bound to the far-reaching technical transformations of the times. The 1880's: the fiasco of General Boulanger's bid for power, his movement completely absorbed by parliamentarianism once the crisis had waned. . . . The 1890's: Méline at the helm supported by the Right. . . . The customary French reaction ensued: political activity of socialism, creation of a leftist majority with anticlericalism as its war horse.

The gradual waning of the crisis after 1900 brought to

the fore a pseudo-parliamentarian stability resting on superficial opposition between parties of the Center: Center Right against Center Left. The extremes were excluded, the extreme Right inclining toward monarchy and the extreme Left aspiring to revolution.

The crisis after World War I brought England true constitutional reform, with the rise of the Labor Party. The French juridical bent, as evident in Edouard Herriot as in Raymond Poincaré, forbade any constitutional reform (with the exception of the action taken by the Millerand presidency, which merely reaffirmed parliamentary liberalism). The Left went no farther than the Cartel of 1924. The Right did not go beyond the rallying of the Radical Party to Poincaré's program. Government by the moderate Center parties remained the rule. Prosperity was worldwide until 1928, in France until 1932. The delay with which France finally experienced depression was due to her Malthusianism, to her very reticence in the face of technical progress.

The world depression of the nineteen thirties created by technical progress was the most formidable crisis yet known. In this instance, the traditional judiciary framework had to give a bit: A rightist authoritarian government was imposed by the riots of February 6, 1934, a government—whoever was its leader—which practically abolished the parliamentary regime, replacing it with government by decree. In accordance with a rhythm existing since 1789, this executive stiffening reminiscent of past monarchical reaction was followed by a counterreaction of a revolutionary type, though it pretended to respect the letter of the constitution, the Popular Front.

Thanks to the definite success of French industrialization in the 1880's, the republican parliamentary regime managed to save face until 1939.

However, the formidable—we purposely repeat this emphatic adjective—worldwide technical advance of the 1930's (Soviet Five Year Plans, New Deal) placed France in a difficult position. To be sure, she had at her command the essential new technical instruments (electricity, aviation, radio, chemistry). Moreover, she was fortunate in that coal no longer played an exclusive role in industrial might. But her political and social structure would not allow her to bear the brunt of brutal shocks. Once again the nonchalance typical of France in the years 1938–1939 contrasted with the ardor of the British and the violence of the Germans.

With the disaster of 1940 the process of oscillation, which had respected the parliamentary constitution with no more than a scratch here and there after 1932, continued. But the swing of the pendulum was unusually strong to the right. In Vichy the old "monarchical" faction anointed Pétain as a sort of king. Symbolically enough he had the blessings of Charles Maurras, the leader of the small yet active Royalist Party.

The oscillating process went on, and in 1944 the pseudo-monarchical rule of Marshal Pétain was replaced by a revolutionary government which allowed Socialists and Communists to impose the reforms required by new technical progress, nationalization of the power industry and of credit.

Then once more the pendulum swung. As soon as the massive progress, from which Vichy had recoiled, had been brutally achieved by the revolutionary presidency of de Gaulle, the regime went back to its routine of handing over the government to the Center. The traditional parties took their old seats in the Chamber of Deputies. The Radical-Socialists again became referees in the seesaw between right and left.

What then of French political instability? Clearly, from 1780 to this day, no country has demonstrated greater constancy in the game of political forces. The basic mechanisms have remained identical for 150 years. What changes is their expression at the surface of political life. What one sees at first sight may appear incoherent; but what one sees less often, the very heart of the matter, is profoundly permanent.

Yes, far more permanent than it is in nations reputed for their stability. The United States, Great Britain, Germany, Italy—none can compare with France with regard to the stability of administrative personnel, in other words, with regard to the stability of the executive infrastructure. The high-ranking executive personnel is incredibly constant; from 1789 to this day it has changed little. This phenomenon has always amazed historians studying the succession of regimes from 1789 to 1815 and from 1815 to 1939. After 1939 the Vichy "purges" ravaged civil service personnel; naturally, this provoked equally ruinous counterpurges during and after the Liberation. Old France had never experienced anything like it. Only recently have the damages done by both sides been somewhat patched up through the progressive reintegration of rightist and leftist elements previously dismissed.

Why such administrative stability? It is partly a reflection of the French inclination toward legality and theory. It stems from an innate respect for the rights of the individual to a government position that he has obtained through solemn examinations and contests. In fact, the respect for intellectual capacity has entailed a yearly increase in the number of government posts open to the successful candidates of the major national contests. Recruitment through competitive examinations was a common procedure in France long before it was adopted by Anglo-Saxon or Germanic countries, and it has taken firmer root in France than anywhere else.

Whereas Britain, the United States, and Germany change the executors if public policy demands it and keep both the regime and the head of the government, France keeps her executors while changing the regime and (ever more frequently) the head of the government. This situation exists because, as Jacques Soustelle recently stated, the regime and the head of the government live at an altitude where the icy winds of "reason of state" blow endlessly —in more prosaic terms, because the government head and the regime are directly exposed to the contrary currents of French passions: the aspirations toward law, science, technical advance, and absolute concepts and also toward heroic and rash adventures.

On the other hand, the executors of public policy are in direct contact with the complexities of French nature; they are rooted in them. Through changing regimes and changing parliamentary majorities, the Ecole Polytechnique continues to control the railroads with a fixity untouched by 130 years of turbulent history. Similarly, each educational institution is at the center of an irreducible, coherent, social group belonging to it—a group from which it draws its future recruits, thereby perpetuating an exclusive frame of mind.

Obviously, French schools have paid for these privileges through outstanding services. They demonstrate a superior capacity to compute theoretically France's needs in the fields they aspire to rule. Because nature in France is more hostile than in other countries, the great schools encounter greater difficulty understanding it. But they have succeeded in creating through devotion to theory that community of ideas and ideals which is precisely the stuff of which coherent social groups are made.

The passion for theory, economic anxiety, and Malthusianism—three of the five characteristic French traits—seem to encourage the development of stable socioeducational groups. (The fact that since Napoleon the Ecole Polytechnique has been attached to the War Ministry stems perhaps from the desire to add the brilliance of authority to the French school system.) The various educational forces existing in France infuse the social complexes they create with a greater measure of authority than that wielded by the government itself.

PART TWO

The Difficulties of the Present

VII

French Power in Tow

ONE cannot exaggerate the part played by the Revolution of 1789 in contemporary French political life—not so much by virtue of what the Revolution may have proclaimed in the past as by what it means to the present. Across the channel political revolutions occurred in the seventeenth century. English precocity was probably due to an insular position which, at an early stage, fostered the commercial and financial social structures most adaptable to technical progress. This very precocity prevented the parliamentary regime of capitalistic industrialization from defining itself once and for all. England's modern political regime largely preceded the mechanization of her economic life.

In France the first signs of mechanization began transforming the social structure *before* the corresponding political institutions were in place. We have already observed that economic events justified revolutionary and military events after 1789, rather than vice versa. Bonaparte succeeded in founding the Bank of France; but, steeped in routine, the steel industry scarcely changed until about 1830.

The government of Louis Philippe was incapable of facing the problems of social and financial reconstruction arising from the establishment of the railroads. In northern France the railroads were rather successful. In the South their progress was insignificant and the first companies either stagnated or failed. The major achievement of the government of Napoleon III was the creation of the great railroad systems and the great shipping companies. Once that crisis in French capitalism had been coped with, the nation went back to parliamentary government.

French colonial enterprises, often quite belatedly, followed the example of their British counterparts, taking advantage of the weakness of non-European countries. Only after 1877 (the constitution of the Third Republic was passed in 1875), did the French political regime provide for the growth of capitalism in the 1900's. This explains the relative constitutional stability of the period.

In the general evolution of the world the depression of 1930 was far more shattering than the usual cyclic crises known to capitalism. It brought in its wake fundamental modifications in the relationships between the state and social and economic life. The United States quickly adopted the New Deal, just as Russia did Stalinism, Brazil Getulism, Germany and Italy their brands of fascism. Britain had already gone through the experience of a socialist government. Among great nations France was the last to adopt a new governmental style. The Popular Front experiment of 1936 was not conclusive, and it failed because it did not dare attempt the economic mobilization of the nation. Not before 1944–1945 did France reform her social and economic structure. This delay is not surprising if we recall that capitalistic social legislation came much later in France than in Britain or Germany. Such are the fruits of French Malthusianism.

The government's tardiness in promoting the necessary structural changes in the nation's economic and social make-up explains the inevitability of brutal political explosions. By definition, parliamentarianism is conceived as a supple system able to adapt to all sorts of new needs. England, for example, progressively substituted Labour for Liberalism.

Why then is the government in France so ill-fitted to renovate the nation's structure? We must remember that the natural coincidence between capitalistic depressions and demographic crises placed France in a position of inferiority. At the precise moment when a major effort was needed to renew her equipment and her society, France saw the number of her young adults suddenly diminish. Exception should be made of the 1890's when immigration brought in new blood.

But this reason is only an expression of a deeper phenomenon: French society is rooted in agrarian, small-town structures. Inspired by the conservatism of its handicraftsmen, it is hostile to credit expansion in capitalistic periods and to planning in socialistic periods. But it is a heady, obstinate conservatism deriving from the natural inadaptability of French geography to modern industrialization. The imbalance is permanent. For as long as she can, France obstinately clings to yesterday's positions; then she veers brutally, attaining new positions in order, once more, to hang on to them in absolute immobility.

The fact is evident in the history of the years 1789 to 1815, 1848 to 1855, 1936 to 1945. Moreover, French parliamentarianism is not alive and dynamic as is that of England: it drags, it hesitates, then it leaps violently by sudden shocks.

In times of crisis the recourse to authoritarian regimes does not mean that the man in power acts as he wishes. He simply presides over the transformations that take place. This was as true in 1802, as in 1850 or 1944-1945.

Real political authority resides in foresight. Yet more than half of the French population refuses to foresee, prefers to hold on to acquired positions. The French regime reflects the same fear of evolution.

Still, the French middle class is one of the strongest in the world, one of the most stable. It develops as much within the framework of old structures and of an antiquated economic psychology as by a more aggressive forward movement. That is properly what distinguishes it from the Anglo-Saxon middle class or the German bourgeoisie. Its inclination toward stability is its fundamental vice. Ordered by the Revolution of 1789, the sudden suppression of the old trade and handicraft corporations was carried out in letter only. The spirit of the artisan has survived with its craving for protective regulations.

Spectacular reforms, generally theoretical and always late, are the fruit of persistency in following economic routines.

It is a jolting sort of game conducive, not to long-term previsions gradually realized, but to cascades of provisional governments. In revolutionary periods governments bear the title "Provisional" with deep pride—for example, as in the years 1944-1945. In periods of constitutional stability they lay claim to scrupulous legality. In either case the government stumbles along. It solemnly points out the peak it is going to reach; but, standing on a sticky clay that holds it fast to the past, it progresses in the irregular manner of an ataxic.

Is it the fault of those who govern? In no other country is the practice of government so difficult, so disappointing. Few nations offer such a contrast between an elite pretending to see far to the future—though disdaining the misfortunes of the present—and a mass faithful to its past.

With what superhuman qualities must a French leader not be endowed? Whereas the British train their few prime ministers over a period of twenty years, French government heads suddenly rise; full of great and noble ideas, they learn reality by direct contact, a reality whose dead weight is unbearable.

The physical environment of French political life is in itself a poor educator. French democracy loves men of modest background. Its main virtue resides in the strongly favorable prejudice it demonstrates toward men whose private lives are patently disinterested and simple. But French democracy houses its leaders in the magnificent gold and velvet of royal palaces. Even the government's furniture is there to remind the new leaders, who arrive burning with generous ideas of progress, that pomp and grandeur are rooted in the past, a past which must be saved. In effect, the very government buildings are lessons in *immobilisme*.

Psychological conditions and exterior trappings transform French political figures into the actors of a tragedy. Is there another nation where power, though tasted ever so fleetingly, has such intoxicating effects? In France the exercise of government breaks the fiber of those charged with it; for, too poor, too small, too loosely knit, the parties have not been able to prepare them for their task through a long, patient, and thorough training.

Parties are an organic part of the parliamentary regime. Only the categorical theorizing typical of French constitutional thought, intent on distinguishing parties from government, could have split in two a political society whose organic unity is an obvious fact. The Anglo-Saxons —after some hesitation on the part of the Americans—were quick to realize this fact. One cannot deny it. To deny it is to reject the parliamentary regime, to prefer traditional monarchy or Caesarism.

Ah, how beautiful the Republic was in the days of the Empire! In France the two-party system has really existed only when a Caesar was in power with the opposition coalesced against him, or else when the entire Right on coming to power abdicated its parliamentary privileges in favor of the executive and by so doing united the Left. Apart from these abnormal cases the system is a multiparty one.

The cause is understandable. For the sake of clarity we shall proceed in two stages.

First, let us consider the Anglo-Saxon two-party system. The alternation in power of Right and Left is possible because there exists a group of independent, undecided voters who hesitate between Right and Left. For the two-party system to survive, it is imperative that these undecided votes not crystallize into a formal party capable of attracting a faithful mass of adherents. The efforts of the two parties always aim at preserving enough strength to stifle the creation of a middle party. The least weakening in the two great parties carries the threat of a new Center party.

In France parties are weak because the parliamentary regime has never won over all of public opinion to its cause. There are in France between six and ten million parliamentary electors whom we shall call *citizens:* three to five million vote to the left (they were supporters of the old Radical Party and now follow socialism), three to five million vote to the right (they support the "moderate" parties). Beyond that, however, there are from six to ten million electors who are resolutely opposed to any form of parliamentary government. Reacting not as *citizens* but as *subjects,* they represent the great majority of the Communist electors and all of the extreme rightists. Given this condition, no vast regrouping can be carried out on the left or on the right. The "floating" votes, characteristic of the independent electors, tend to crystallize into a central party which acts as a flail. According to circumstances, this crystallization is more or less well defined. It can be complete around a Radical Party nucleus or broken up and hesitant among several nuclei (the Radical Party on one hand, diverse parties created by the Resistance, on the other hand: Social-Republicans [Gaullists], Union Démocratique et Sociale de la Résistance (UDSR), and a fraction of the MRP).

In any case, the French political picture comprises at least five differing elements. Following a well-established sociological process, this heterogeneity entails the heterogeneity of each party. The French political game is always played by a fivesome. We shall review their respective positions.

The extreme Right is conservative. Does it represent great fortunes? No, rather moderate and small incomes. It is inspired by a nostalgia for the monarchical protections of the past: corporatism, state organization of production and distribution. Defending the aged structures dear to craftsmen and peasants, it continues to doubt the virtues and even the very validity of technical progress. It rejects

THE FRENCH AND THE REPUBLIC

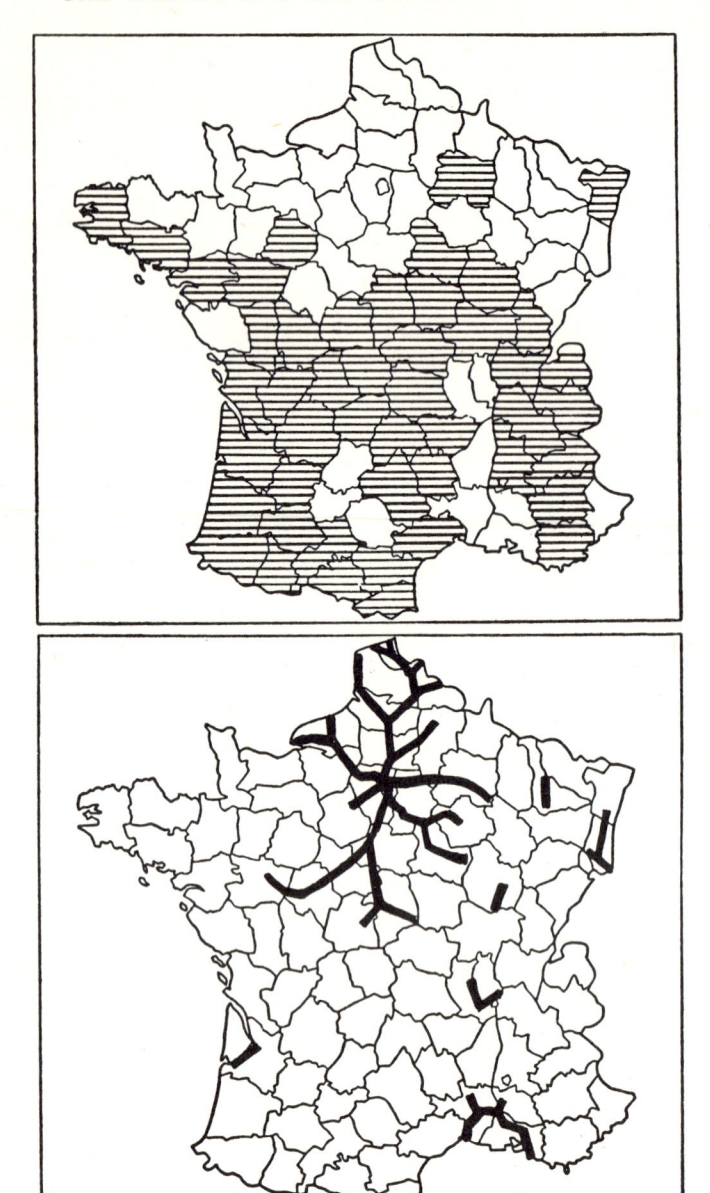

FIGURE 8

the "Anglicizing" of France. Unaffected by juridical subtleties, it readily violates law and order in the name of country and property. Not particularly inclined toward theory, it shows a nostalgia for religion and a love of adventure.

The Center Right believes in technical progress (more than in scientific progress, as a matter of fact); but it measures the historical difficulties opposing progress in France and is led to doubt the possibility of implementing it. It is generally resigned to the practice of economic Malthusianism while eloquently professing its anti-Malthusianism. We have already noted that in France this declaration of principle is not concretely observed. It is frequently inclined toward religion, but it fears adventure. Lastly, it leans heavily on law and right.

The Center Left prides itself on a favorable disposition toward scientific and technical progress. Indeed, it willingly associates scientists with its political action. In this manner, it extols a lay philosophy which is transformed into a sort of positivistic religion. In economic matters it treads cautiously in the fear of extreme measures. Though it actively combats economic Malthusianism, it is far less aggressive in its opposition to demographic Malthusian-

---

FIGURE 8. Abstentions from Voting in 1928 (*upper*); Railways about 1848 (*lower*).

Blank areas indicate abstentions fewer than 17% of registered voters; lined areas, abstentions more than 17%.

In indicating the high degree of participation in legislative elections this figure shows that the France of 1928 was still the France of the old liberal regimes. Where the railways were successfully established before the Revolution of 1848, voters eighty years later still appreciated the parliamentary regime. The Parisian region and its extensions to the north and, on the other hand, Lyons and the Rhone Valley are regions firmly won over to parliamentary government.

THE FRENCH AND THE REPUBLIC

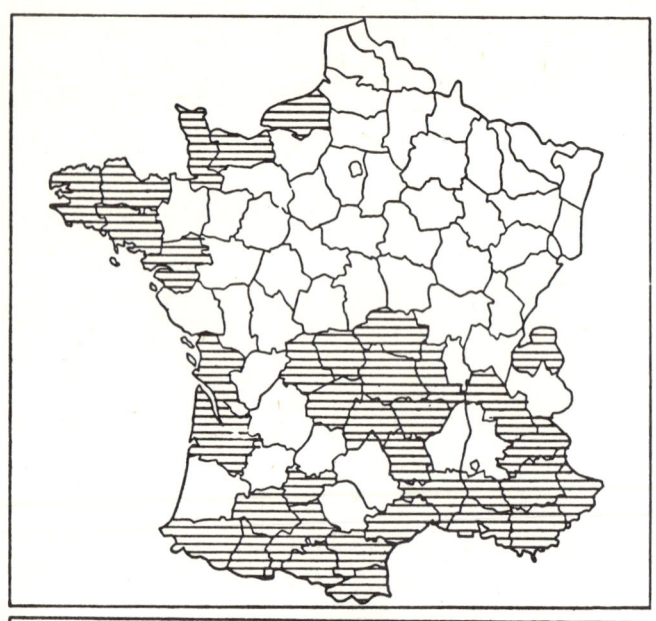

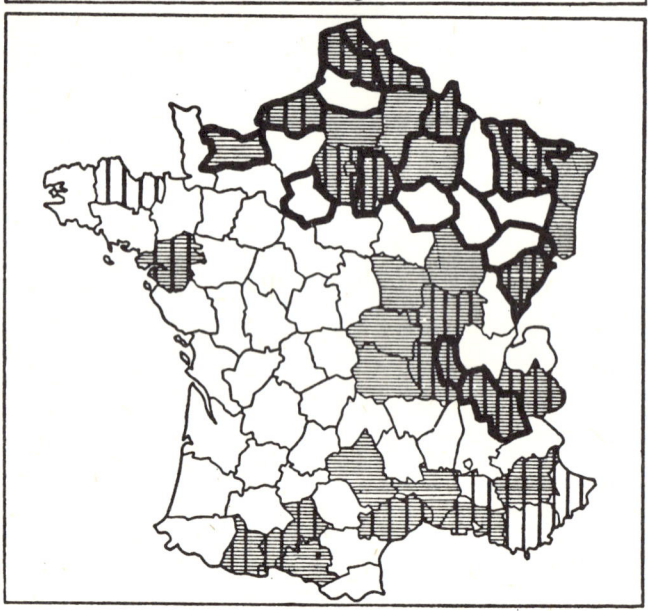

FIGURE 9

ism. It also evinces a strong attachment to law, but it is essentially motivated by a desire to protect the integrity of law. It demonstrates little inclination for adventure.

The extreme Left prides itself on its doctrine and its theoretical principles, which are, in fact, the most coherent and the best adapted to the progressive point of view. It makes a determined effort to attract scientists and technicians. It distrusts legality, considering it a factor of economic and social stagnation. By definition it is anti-Malthusian. It has no calling toward economic prudence and exploits as best it can the French inclination toward revolutionary adventures.

What brings the two Lefts together is their rejection of Malthusianism and their preference for science over religion. What brings the two Rights together is a Malthusian desire to preserve vested interests (not only those of the wealthy, but also of the poor and middle classes). What brings the two Centers together is their economic prudence, their concern for legality.

There remains the fifth element in our picture, the real

FIGURE 9. Abstentions from Voting in 1956 (*upper*); Income about 1954 (*lower*).

Map at top: blank areas—abstentions fewer than 17% of the registered voters; lined areas—abstentions more than 17%.

Map at bottom: blank areas—wages of a majority less than 250,000 francs a year; areas with horizontal lines—more than 250,000 francs a year. Areas marked by vertical lines—wages of 5.2% between 500,000 and 800,000 francs a year; areas bordered in heavy black—average income per taxpayer above 410,000 francs.

Twenty-eight years later the new industrialization bringing higher incomes and coinciding with the success of the labor parties (see Figure 13 lower) has led a few new districts to a higher voting average. Industry in the Southeast has made forward strides. Communism is developing in parliamentary regions (see Figure 10 lower), which is a further indication that communism is becoming parliamentary minded, the Communist Party having already participated in the governments of 1945 and 1946.

THE FRENCH AND THE REPUBLIC

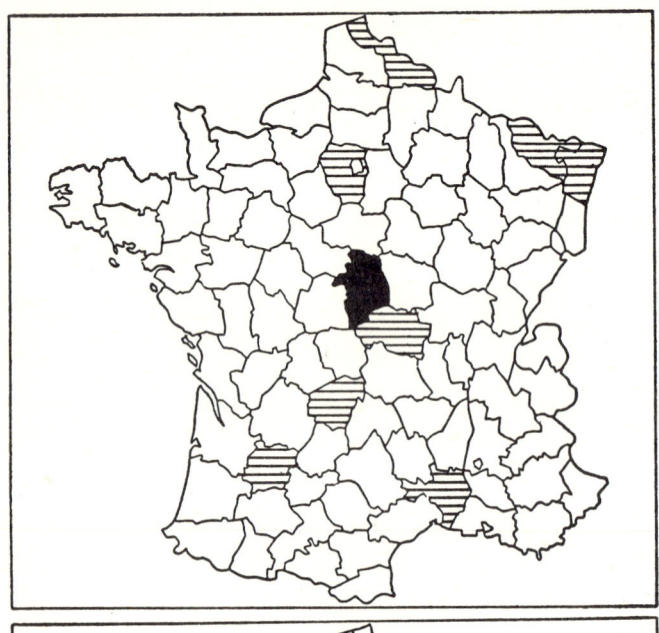

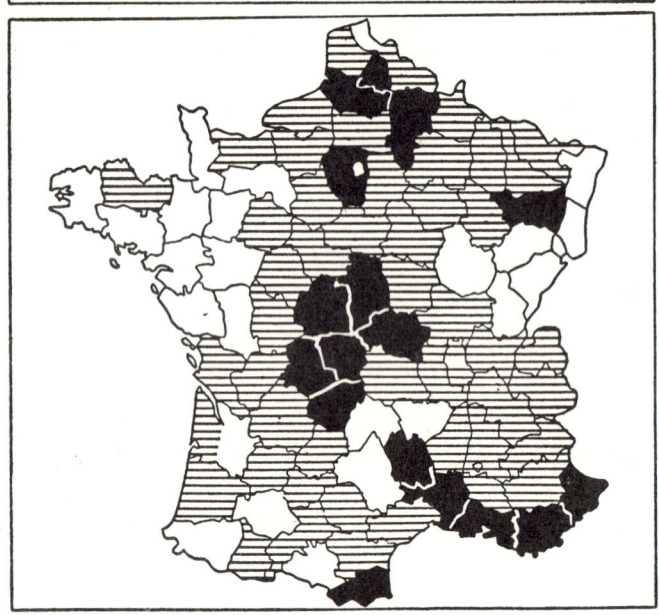

FIGURE 10

Center. It adopts all the tendencies mentioned, combining them into varying patterns according to the times and the idiosyncrasies of its small parties. It is impossible here to analyze the infinite variety of these combinations. We shall simply outline the essential points.

At the beginning of the Third Republic the Radical Party belonged to the Left. Its goal then was to substitute an ethic of progress for the traditionally Catholic way of life of old France. The steady rise of the Socialist Party sent the Radicals drifting to the right, for the Socialists were partisans of the total reform of property laws, while the Radicals were committed to their preservation. The development of communism had a twofold effect: it led the Socialists to take on the role of a labor party and to accept the parliamentary regime; it carried the Radicals to the very center of the French political picture.

After 1924 it became impossible to govern without the Radical Party, henceforth the arbiter of the nation's political action. It incarnates the French version of parliamentary government. In economic and legal matters it frequently espouses the policies of the Right. Yet its theoretical stand on matters of science and techniques, its avowed lay philosophy, bring it in harmony with the Left. Its very essence is to vary according to circumstance.

Necessary as early as 1930 and finally achieved by the government of Liberation, the nationalization of banks,

---

FIGURE 10. Communists in 1928 (*upper*) and 1956 (*lower*).

Black areas—Communist vote more than 25% of the registered voters; lined areas—more than 15%.

Communism from its very beginning settled at the heart of France, in a zone where attempts to create a British type of industry had failed. This central zone started moving southeast, while the spots along the northern and southern borders were developing considerably.

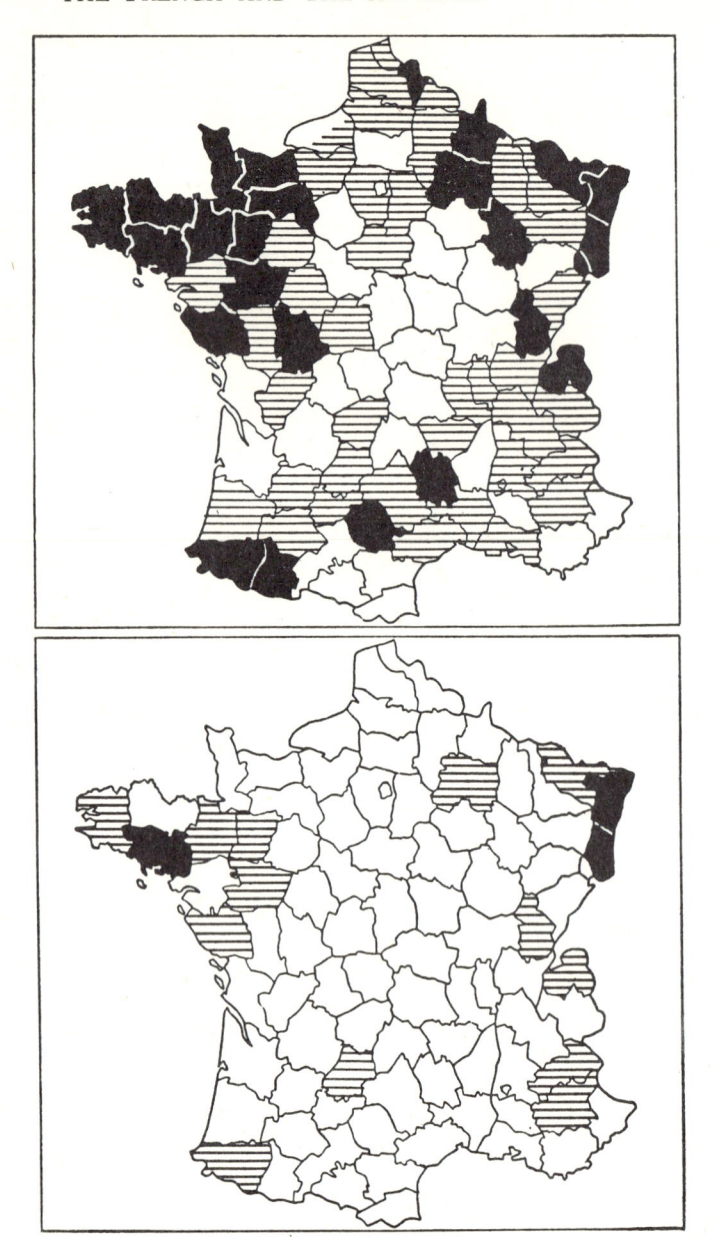

FIGURE 11

power, and key industries was a cruel blow to the Radical Party. At the time of the government of Liberation a compact majority knit by the Resistance movement had succeeded in passing massive legislation establishing nationalization and a social security system including socialized medicine and other forms of individual and family protection. Confronted by this wave of ambitious reforms, the Radical Party remained faithful to the traditions of nineteenth-century liberalism and slid rightward. This move to the right lasted until the necessary structural reforms of the nation's economic and social condition had been accomplished.

The economic Malthusianism practiced by the French from 1919 to 1939 discredited the old liberalism for a while. It was only through a vast regrouping by the state of the nation's financial equipment that reconstruction, modernization, and the development of energy were possible. This need so eclipsed all others that the traditional quarrel between church and state was set aside.

Radicalism, whose bonds with the Left consisted in a common lay point of view and whose bonds with the Right consisted in financial orthodoxy, could no longer pretend it belonged to the Center. The MRP took over its place. The MRP's religious faith, the support it receives from

---

FIGURE 11. Mouvement Républicain Populaire (MRP) in 1946 and 1956.

Black areas—MRP votes more than 25% of the registered voters; lined areas—more than 15%.

Regrouping the interests of the Center Right and mustering the anti-Marxist forces, the MRP of 1946 fought communism with its own favorite weapons: nationalizations and social security. Once the major structural reforms had been accomplished, the MRP became more regional. Except in periods of economic revolution, the right to power is denied to the advocates of religious education.

THE FRENCH AND THE REPUBLIC

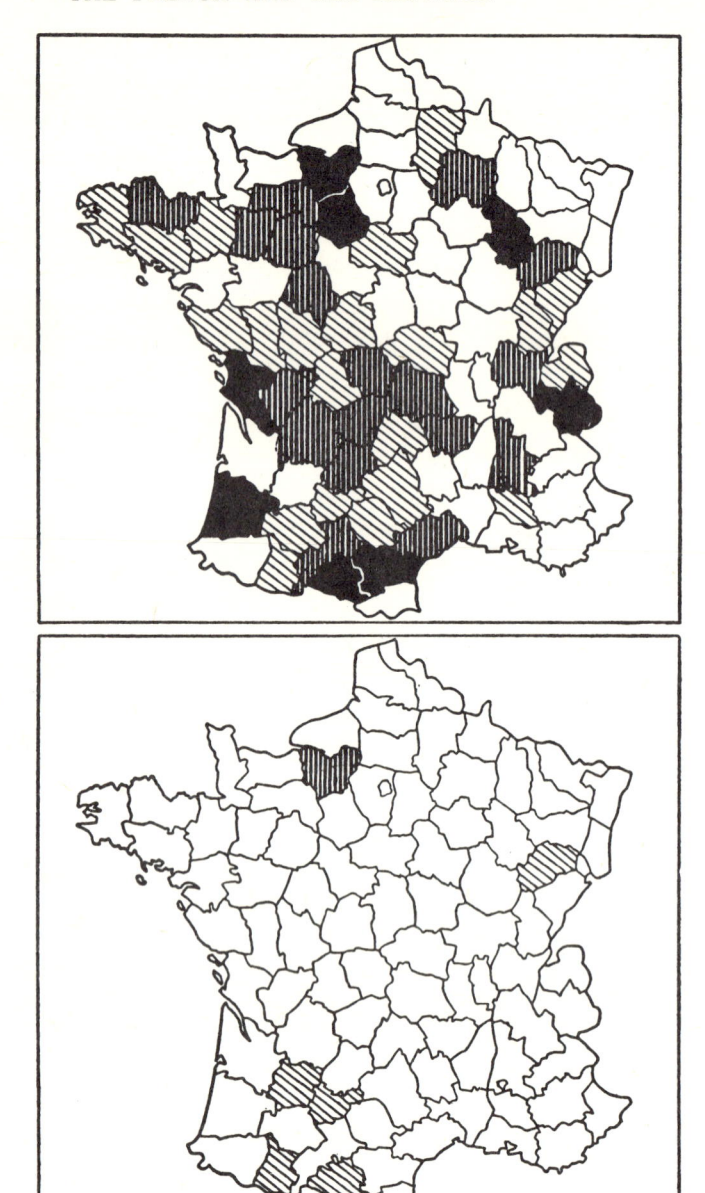

FIGURE 12

the Catholic hierarchy, tie it to the Right. Its syndicalism and its understanding of necessary structural reforms tie it to the Left. So long as the question of church and state remains dormant, the MRP can assume the role of a Center party.

Consequently, after 1944 the MRP was able to attract the independent floating votes—as the Radical Party had been able to do before the war. It fulfilled the same position as arbiter between parties and supplier of the nation's prime ministers. Its direct and indirect influence on administrative personnel was on the rise. For the first time in many years the church was thwarting freemasonry.

Still, the victory of the MRP was not as lasting as that of the Christian-Democrat parties of Germany and Italy (see Figure 19). The stabilizing of world prices brought a return to financial orthodoxy, thereby, infusing new life in the Radical Party. The appearance of the Gaullist RPF threatened to sever the MRP from the Right unless it became a more determined champion of subsidies to the parochial schools. In short, the MRP was forced toward

---

FIGURE 12. The Radicals in 1928 (*upper*) and the Radicals plus the Union Démocratique et Socialiste de la Résistance in 1956 (*lower*).

Black areas—Radical vote more than 35% of the registered voters; vertically lined areas—Radical (or Radical plus USDR) vote more than 30%; obliquely lined areas—more than 25%.

In 1928 the Radicals held strong positions of two different types: in the Parisian region, a zone of classical parliamentarianism, they made up the liberal Left of a two-party system; in the South and the West, pseudo-parliamentary zones, they formed the center of a five-party system.

The party's severe contraction can be explained in the following way: it found itself carried to the right of the French political scene from 1944 to 1946; then it turned down an opportunity to regain a central position in 1955 in the hope of erasing any memory of its previous association with the Right.

THE FRENCH AND THE REPUBLIC

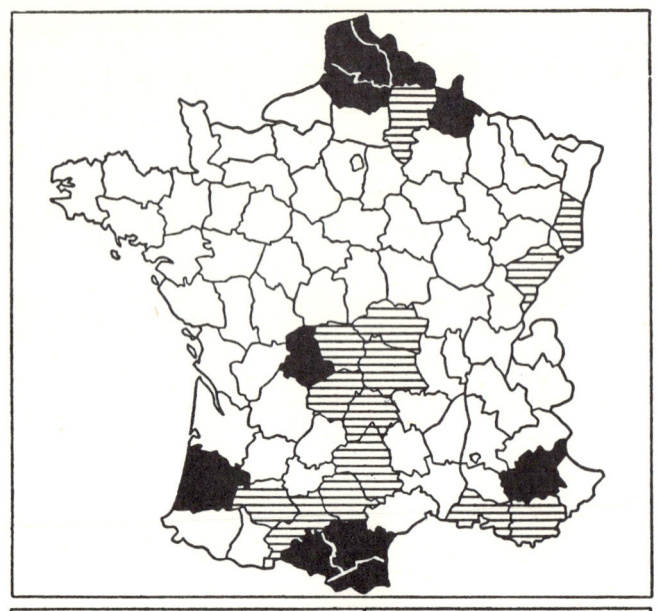

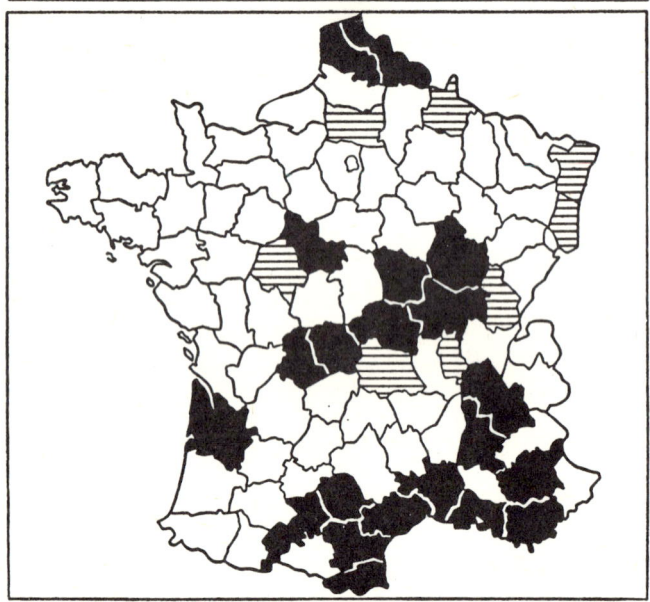

Figure 13

the right; the center changed hands, returning once again to its previous occupants, the Radical Party.

In ten years, then, the Center changed incumbents at least twice. And so far we have discussed only two parties. In reality, there are three or four milling about the center. When a grave problem arises in Britain, the two great parties define their respective positions and ask the independent voters to choose between them. In France parties to the left and, above all, to the right entrench themselves in traditional positions becoming prisoners of their own political personality. On the right, through lack of interest, there is no significant effort to inform and educate the elector. The Center Left, particularly the Socialist Party, demonstrates good will, earnestness, and zeal; but its means are limited, its methods of education at times too dogmatic. Only the Communists really educate their electors, or rather, indoctrinate them. To summarize, French electors are not educated by their parties; they are not given the opportunity to exercise a clear choice.

Problems are merely aggravated by this condition. And it is at such times that the various fractions of the center prove most active. Three or four parties, or elements of parties, try to win the election by transforming their own programs or by fighting among themselves to lure the inde-

---

FIGURE 13. Socialists in 1928 (*upper*) and 1956 (*lower*).

Black areas—Socialist vote more than 20% of the registered voters; lined areas—more than 15%.

In 1918, though it had been forced to give up Berry, socialism still offered the geographical picture of an extreme leftist movement. By 1956 socialism in the North had strengthened its position by turning into a labor party on the British pattern. By this very fact it accepted the parliamentary regime. In the South, where a labor party on the British pattern would not be capable of adapting to the peculiar environment, socialism tends to take over the positions left vacant by the Radical Party.

THE FRENCH AND THE REPUBLIC

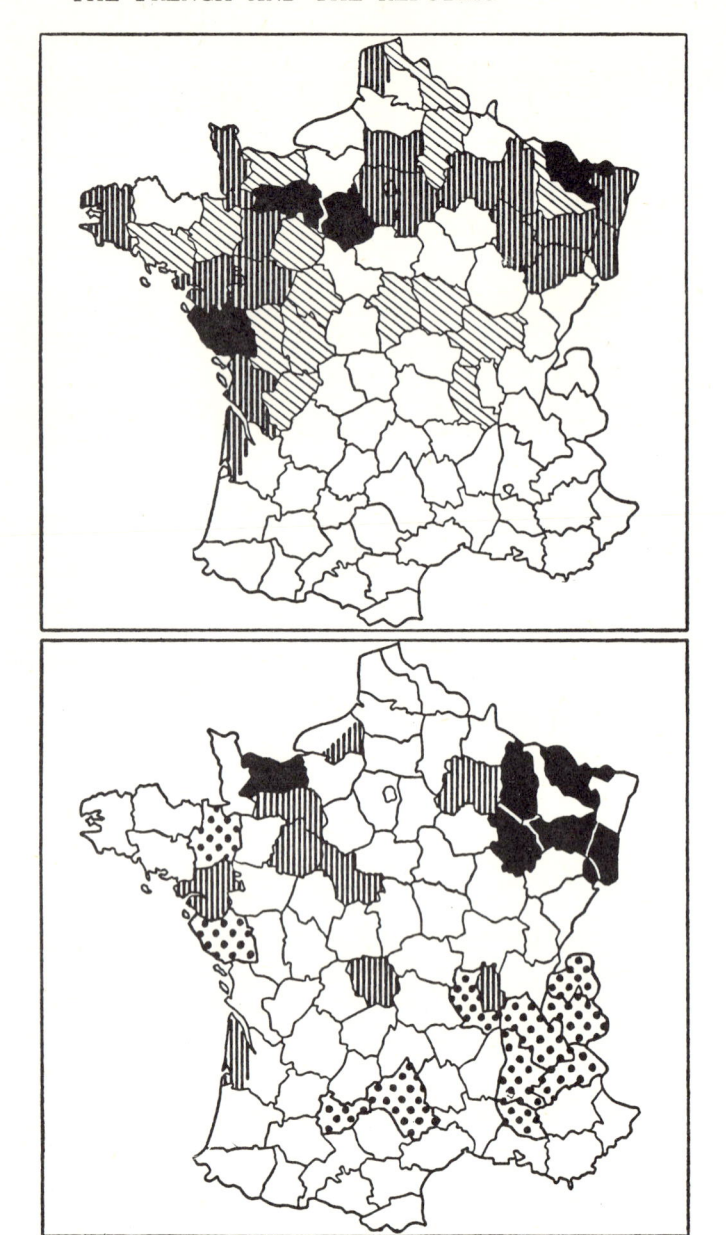

FIGURE 14

pendent voter. Obviously, then, an election is not won, as in England, by a veritable tidal wave, but simply by the gain of a few Center votes. Thus, new circumstances give birth to a new Center. Normally the operation will only affect a small proportion of the electoral body and a small number of the deputies of the National Assembly. The elector's decision will not be clear-cut; the re-education of the electorate and of the deputies will not be significant.

In France a problem must reach a rare degree of gravity for a true electoral decision to be manifested. That is why the dissolution of the National Assembly cannot fulfill the same role that dissolution of Parliament does in England. As soon as two or three urgent questions appear, divisions occur within each party, particularly in the center, and the opposition between parties rapidly reaches a climax. In this troubled atmosphere it is futile to expect a clear choice by the voter. The surprise election of 1956 is a case in point; it registered the general confusion with photographic precision instead of offering some manner of remedy.

The incapacity of the French parliamentary regime to obtain a clear electoral verdict obliges the center parties

---

FIGURE 14. Rassemblement du Peuple Français (RPF) in 1951 (*upper*); Communist Gains and Losses, 1951–1956 (*lower*).

Upper map: Black areas—RPF vote more than 30% of the registered voters; vertically lined areas—more than 20%; obliquely lined areas—more than 15%.

Lower map: Black areas—more than 20% gain; lined areas—more than 15% gain; dotted areas—losses.

The geographical picture of the RPF reveals that it is associated with the classical Right in the West, while it becomes the expression of a curiously original movement in the modern industrial zone of the East. It had little opportunity to show itself in the Vichy "Free Zone" from 1940 to 1944. Its withdrawal eastward is accompanied by Communist gains.

THE FRENCH AND THE REPUBLIC

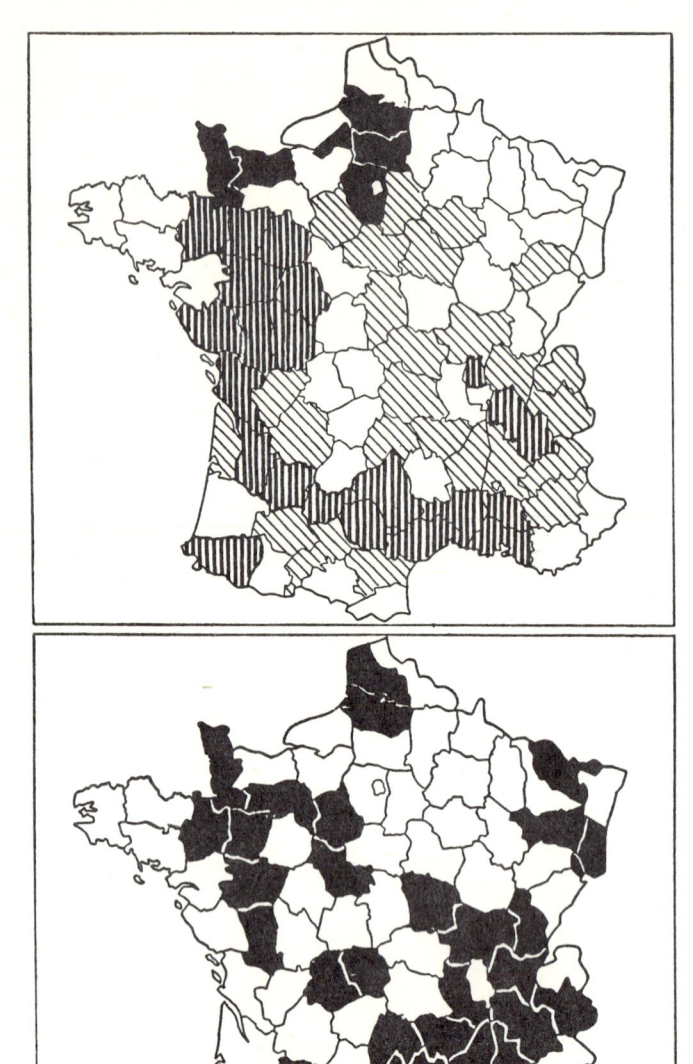

FIGURE 15

to take decisive steps with or without the consent of their electors. Further, the more the center parties adapt their programs to the needs of the day—at the price, consequently, of breaking yesterday's electoral promises—the more loudly opponents on the right and the left boast of loyalty to their own programs and practice a merely negative education of public opinion, rather than engage in a useful clarification of the new situation.

Hence the fragile nature of parliamentary majorities and the frequency of ministerial crises. Hence the length of crises; long, because the Right and the Left proceed to a slow and overparticular choice between the different possible solutions offered by the Center.

And so decisions are put off, delayed, halfheartedly introduced, until the day when a political problem becomes a political drama—until the day when events accomplish what parties do so poorly, the education of the government, of the deputies, and of public opinion. Then, very suddenly, a heterogeneous majority is formed.

It is not the symptoms of a crisis which impose governments of action, but the crisis itself, experienced with a nearly catastrophic intensity. In such an atmosphere, obviously, governments come to power too late, too ill-prepared for the harassing decisions that must be made.

FIGURE 15. The Right and Poujade, 1956 (*upper*); Increases in Revenue (*lower*).

Upper map: Black areas—rightist vote more than 10% of the registered voters; vertical lines—Poujade more than 15%; oblique lines—Poujade more than 10%.

Lower map: Black areas—increase in income between 1938 and 1946 more than 9%.

The geographical spread of the Poujade movement is quite different from that of the RPF. In the most backward zones, where income increases only in periods of extreme rightist economy (Vichy) and of great inflation (1943–1946), extreme rightist discontent has replaced extreme leftist discontent.

The most imperative problems are met by hasty improvisation and jolting measures. Once the absolutely essential steps have been taken, the public reproaches its men of action for having reneged on their electoral promises. Yet how could they do otherwise? The heterogeneous majority starts falling apart; the country returns to *immobilisme;* the game goes on.

This characteristic of French governments springs from the very personality of the country—a most complex country, where firm choices lead to its division.

FIGURE 16. The Governments of the Fourth Republic.

The rectangles are proportionate in size to the number of deputies.
The black is proportionate to the number of abstentions or to the nay votes at the time of investiture in office.
The white expresses the yea votes at the time of investiture in office.
The figures represent the number of ministers per party in the government.
The name is that of the Prime Minister.
The gray is proportionate in size to the duration of the government below which it appears.
Divers—other parties; div. dr.—other parties on the right.

This chart shows how the precious center positions, which are a government's backbone, are won and lost.

From 1946 to 1948 the MRP was *the* center party and acted as the arbiter of the political scene. Thanks to its laborite policies, the MRP succeeded in pushing classical radicalism to the right.

But after 1950, breaking away from the Socialists, the MRP offered the Radicals a chance to recover power and to return to the center of the political arena.

The intervention of the RPF in January 1952 gave its opportunity to the Center Right, and to Laniel, who not so long before had been the leader of the PRL (Parti Républicain de la Liberté) and as such had been relegated to isolation on the extreme right.

In June 1954 the Radical Party recovered its place in the center. This came after the Center Right had borne the blame for the disaster at Dien Bien Phu. The Radicals now rallied the Left, thus forming a paradoxical majority in an Assembly which the RPF had stretched out further to the right.

From this came the divisions in the ranks of the Radicals, the return to a Center Right majority, the dissolution of the Assembly underlining the failure of the various Centers, and the return to a Center Left majority reminiscent of the situation in 1947.

FRENCH POWER IN TOW

First Constituent Assembly Jan. 26, 1946	Comm 146	S.F.I.O 143	M.R.P 139	R.G.R 37	PRL 20	Divers 75
Second Constituent Assembly April 26, 1946	Comm. 153	S.F.I.O. 127	M.R.P. 169	R.G.R. 49	PRL 70	Div 18
First Legislature	Comm. 183	S.F.I.O. 102	M.R.P. 154	R.G.R. 68	Div.Dr. 53 PRL 34	Div 22

Dec. 16, 1946		BLUM 18				
Jan. 28, 1947	5	RAMADIER 9	5	5	2	
May 6, 1947		RAMADIER 9	5	5	2	
Nov. 27, 1947		5	SCHUMAN 5	3	1	
July 26, 1948		5	6	MARIE 6	2	
Sept. 8, 1948			SCHUMAN			

117

Sept. 13, 1948 | 4 | 5 | QUEUILLE 4 | 1

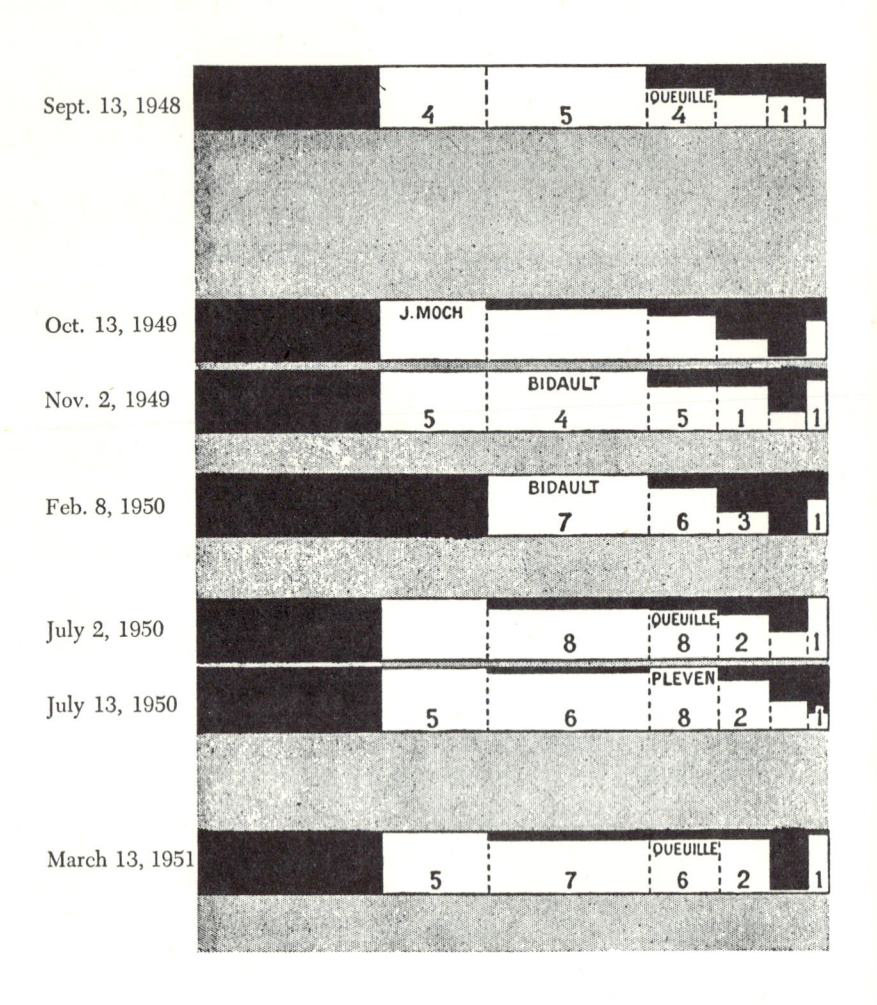

Oct. 13, 1949 | J. MOCH

Nov. 2, 1949 | 5 | BIDAULT 4 | 5 | 1 | 1

Feb. 8, 1950 | BIDAULT 7 | 6 | 3 | 1

July 2, 1950 | 8 | QUEUILLE 8 | 2 | 1

July 13, 1950 | 5 | 6 | PLEVEN 8 | 2 | 1

March 13, 1951 | 5 | 7 | QUEUILLE 6 | 2 | 1

FRENCH POWER IN TOW

Second Legislature	Comm. 103	S.F.I.O. 104	M.R.P. 85	R.G.R. 94	Divers Droite 98	R.P.F. 118	Divers 23
Aug. 8, 1951			7	PLEVEN 9	7		
Jan. 17, 1952			8	FAURE 10	8		
March 6, 1952			4	7	PINAY 5		
Jan. 6, 1953			6	MAYER 9	7		
June 22, 1953			4	6	LANIEL 5	3	
June 17, 1954			1	MENDÈS-F. 8	4	4	
Feb. 23, 1955			4	FAURE 6	5	4	

Third Legislature	Comm. 150	S.F.I.O. 95	Rad. 77	Rép. Soc. 21	M.R.P. 83	Div. Dr. 109	Pouj. 51	Div. 6
Feb. 2, 1956		MOLLET 6	6					

VIII

From Provisional Government to Chance Government

FOR several months in 1944–1945 France had a regime which was a combination of its three traditional regimes. The misery that then prevailed, born of the great misfortunes of those years, prevented opinion at large from measuring the perfection of that triple combination—a combination made possible by the very gravity of the situation.

For once the nation's confidence went out to a president whose authority was not founded on universal suffrage but on the strength of his own foresight, Charles de Gaulle. For once the nation was endowed with that power of prevision and wise counsel which it so often lacks. It was the power of a single man—in other words, an extreme right style of government.

But also it was an extreme left type of government, for all the practical decisions had been carefully prepared by a small insurrectional committee, the National Committee for the Resistance (CNR).

Indeed, the coexistence of these two styles of government is a rare event in France. Normally, they follow one another without any sort of overlapping.

Furthermore, regular parliamentary government was reinstated with the election of the First Constituent Assembly immediately after the war.

This triple regime was too extraordinary to last. The parliamentary mind is just as suspicious of the extreme Right's style of government as it is of the extreme Left's. To be sure, the parliamentary regime found 30 per cent of the nation opposed to its revival. But the alternative, government by the extreme Right or by the extreme Left, would have aroused the hostility of 80 per cent of the electoral body. Charles de Gaulle could not help but sense the suspicion directed against him from the moment the debates started in the newly elected Assembly. Moreover, the elections had rendered the authority of the Resistance and of its various organs obsolete.

Finally, de Gaulle, so brilliantly prophetic in his analysis of the world from 1930 to 1944, seems to have hesitated after 1944 in the face of a situation dominated by the questions of the Far East and of the Moslem world. His authority rested on infallibility. Should the latter temporarily escape him, he would again be controlled by the authority of universal suffrage.

Had General de Gaulle already contemplated appealing his case to the electoral body in January 1946 when he rendered his famous and faithful accounts? In any event, his ties with the extreme Left weighed upon him, just as did the resurgence of traditional parliamentarianism. Taking the nation by surprise, he resigned.

French parliamentary government was back in power. And once more, it took its bearings from the Center.

The years 1944–1946 marked the reign of the tripartism: Communists, Socialists, and MRP agreed on essential structural reforms. The MRP then formed the right of the regime and the Socialists the center. Significantly, Félix Gouin, General de Gaulle's successor, belonged to that new center by virtue of his allegiance to the Socialist Party.

When the economic and social situations became more normal, when nationalizations had been enacted, the parties representative of orthodox liberalism reawakened. This forced the Socialist Party back to the left and the central position was occupied by the MRP. As early as June 1946 Georges Bidault, leading member of the MRP, was carried to the premiership of the Provisional Government. This was the time of nearly unanimous votes of investiture for designated Prime Ministers—only a small, irreducible extreme Right ever voiced dissent—and there was some hesitation in the choice between a Socialist or a member of the MRP: after Georges Bidault, two Socialists became heads of the government, Léon Blum and Paul Ramadier.

For two years the Communists shared the responsibility of power and tacitly accepted the parliamentary regime. The Communist Party even campaigned in favor of productivity, urging industrial workers to produce and encouraging them to accept sacrifices with all the more ardor that communism enjoyed greater popular backing than it had before the war. The Communist Party also devoted much energy to promoting the vast program of French social security. But its attitude started wavering when a government placed in office by nearly unanimous vote of the National Assembly undertook to resist the Vietminh in Indochina while supporting the development of non-Communist unions in France. After the Moscow Conference of March 1947, the Right and the Center took alarm at Stalin's rejection of France's claims to the coal fields of the Saar. And on May 6, 1947, the Communist ministers were ousted by decree from a government to which their party and they themselves had refused confidence (by strict parliamentary procedure the Communist ministers should of course have resigned).

This turn of events shifted the government toward the right. Paul Ramadier was the last Socialist Prime Minister until Guy Mollet became Prime Minister nearly ten years later. The government reverted to the MRP with Robert Schuman, then went further to the right, to the Radical Party, with André Marie. From that date on only the Radical Party and the MRP could lay claim to the premiership, and Georges Bidault and Henri Queuille became the protagonists.

During the first National Assembly the MRP stood out statistically as the great hinge party. But the political repercussions of the Communist Party's return to systematic opposition carried the premiership into the hands of the Radicals. This ambiguity brought with it a realignment of parties, a regrouping which presented few obstacles since the halt in nationalization had detached the MRP from its allies on the left. Then the old quarrels over the parochial schools resumed a political significance that they had lost during the four preceding years. The Catholic loyalty of the MRP forced it to the right. Although it had lost many supporters and much of its prewar prestige, the Radical Party recovered its position as *the* center party: rightist in its attachment to economic liberalism, leftist in its lay philosophy.

These conditions prevailed in 1951 when the election campaigns for the second National Assembly were being prepared. A phenomenon of great importance then intervened—the establishment of de Gaulle's Rassemblement du Peuple Français. Its relative success in 1951 saddled Parliament with a seemingly irreducible Right, just as it had been burdened since 1947 with an irreducible Left. In the center rose what Léon Blum had called the "Third Force." The Socialists at first supported a center government presided over by René Pleven, who had briefly held power during the winter of 1950–1951 and was a leader of the UDSR.

The UDSR is a strange political formation. By vocation a center party, it was born during the Resistance. It represents the remains of a vast, ephemeral, and fragile regrouping which had hoped to organize all the men of good will belonging to the Resistance. But at the Liberation Communists and Socialists had recovered their own troops. On the other hand, the MRP, a competitor also born of the Resistance, had found sturdy support in the church, in the Christian labor unions, and in the Catholic Youth movement. The MRP had the advantage of claiming as its own Georges Bidault, president of the CNR (Comité National de la Résistance). In every respect the MRP seemed singled out to combat communism. In short, the UDSR was reduced to a small group of men displaying various tendencies; their style was reminiscent of the Radicals' but their position was enhanced by the prestige of the Resistance. René Pleven, an ex-Gaullist who had joined the UDSR, was better suited than a classic member of the Radical Party to confront General de Gaulle's newly created RPF. He it was, then, who became Prime Minister.

Once the Gaullists had been checked, once economic and social reforms had been brought to a halt, the second National Assembly revived the traditions of the Third

Republic; the Radicals became essentially the governmental party. As a result Edgar Faure, one of their youngest members, came to power in January 1952 with one major political objective, to convert the RPF deputies to the parliamentary regime.

To understand this objective, we must sum up the meaning of the years that have followed the Liberation and consider them in the light of France's political evolution since the machine age.

English parliamentary procedure tends to have a *total* Right succeed a *total* Left within the framework of the same constitutional system. Now in France, whenever similar successions take place, the constitution is usually transformed. The Popular Front government was a *total* Left government possessing pseudo-revolutionary characteristics. It succeeded the *total* Right government presided over by Doumergue, which in itself possessed pseudo-authoritarian characteristics. Both were on the borderline of constitutional modifications (the Doumergue plan of reform, the Blum project of reform). The government of 1940–1944 was a total Right government; it secreted a monarchical constitution. The governments of 1944 to May 1947 were governments of the total Left. During those three years France was given three regimes: an insurrectional one with a pseudo-revolutionary provisional government, a government by a single Assembly, and the present system.

If one had imagined that this strong swing from total Left to total Right would continue after the break with communism and the cooling off of the Socialists, the hour in 1951–1952 might have seemed ripe for a total Right government to take over and reform the constitution. Such was precisely the avowed objective of the RPF. General de Gaulle, a leader with the temperament of a rightist, happened, by force of events, to have previously presided over the most leftist government the Republic had known, so that when he threw his RPF against the Communists, he practically rallied only the extreme Right and the Center Right.

We have already observed that these swings from total Right to total Left are made possible by the conjunction of financial crises and low birth rates. It happened that 1948–1956 was a period characterized both by relative capitalistic stability and by an increased birth rate. As a result, the RPF, unable to gain sufficient ground to the left and to the center, was pushed into the extreme right of the Assembly. Could it not be lured back into the parliamentary game?

As we have noted, periods of relative capitalistic and demographic stability always coincide in France with government by the Center. Since 1948 Center governments have held forth. But Center Left or Center Right? The RPF still had a chance. Normal in periods of comparative financial insecurity, government by the Center Left would have been anomalous in the spring of 1952—at a time when prices were stable and when postwar reconversion appeared to be successful enough in capitalistic countries. Social and economic conditions, therefore, weighed heavily in favor of the Center Right. After a short crisis Antoine Pinay, spokesman of a small Center Right party, became Prime Minister. The attraction of power, the ambition of action, were strong enough to cut an important portion of the RPF deputies away from their antiparliamentary program.

From then on the "Orleanist" Right or the Radical Right had a firm grip on power (successively, Antoine Pinay,

René Mayer, and Joseph Laniel). From then on, abandoning their leader, de Gaulle, and the principles of their party, nearly all of the RPF deputies were swept into the parliamentary game—a game which would have continued indefinitely along the center right axis ("center" because most of the RPF had in fact renounced any intention of reforming the constitution) had it not been for the Indochinese crisis (coinciding with a minor economic crisis), which for eight months hoisted the Center Left to power in the person of Pierre Mendès-France.

It is absurd to suppose that General de Gaulle could then have inspired a different attitude in the RPF than the one chosen. Nevertheless, we might consider the following hypothesis, no matter how absurd. If the RPF has said, "Forget the institutions; first change the men and their political habits," while it would have lost the support of the parliamentary regime's traditional enemies, it would have established itself at the very center of the political game at the expense of the MRP, of the Radical Party, and of the UDSR. In short, it would have emerged as the arbiter of the situation.

Instead, by deliberately placing itself in opposition to the regime, the RPF spared the various Centers, swallowed part of the Right, and despite its hostility toward the Communists, became their ally in the effort to destroy the existing political system. Nor were the RPF deputies able to remain loyal to their program. Once in contact with parliamentary government their hostility rapidly cooled. Most of them moved away from the party, or at least refused to adopt their leader's intransigence. The RPF's political vocation was dual. As a rightist movement, it lost deputies who joined forces with Antoine Pinay's Independent and Peasant Party. As a movement of political renovation, it conserved a group of loyal members who, increasingly embarrassed by their silent alliance with the Communists, were gradually inclined to seek reform from *within* the existing framework rather than to impose it from *without*. The RPF disappeared as an organized party; its more "loyal" members became the Social-Republicans (*Republicains-sociaux*). These "loyal" elements took a center position early in 1953—a position which, if adopted in 1947, might possibly have carried General de Gaulle to power, but which, in 1953, assuredly led the Social-Republicans to be among the most active participants of the Fourth Republic. Because of this participation they were justified in 1956 in leaving their seats on the extreme right and moving to the center of the Assembly, close to the MRP, the UDSR, and the Radicals. By then there were at least four separate center parties: MRP, Radicals, Social-Republicans, and UDSR.

Since 1789 a center party has been burdened by a heavy liability, the obligation of changing opinions according to circumstances. The Social-Republicans have lent themselves to this difficult role. The most famous of them, General Koenig, once he became Minister of War, completely forgot General de Gaulle's recommendations for the creation of a professional army; he even collaborated in overseas policies scarcely compatible with those held by de Gaulle in June 1940. Participating in governments of the Center Left (Mendès-France) and of the Center Right (Edgar Faure), General Koenig made it a point of honor firmly to oppose the European Defense Community (EDC); yet, though an enemy of the 1951 electoral law, he owes his re-election in 1956 to the 1951 law enabling him to enter into an alliance with the MRP —the very party that invented the EDC and has remained its most faithful champion. All of this, without a single word being pronounced in the National Assembly; for, in truth, it was taken for granted that General Koenig's attitude was not dictated by "personal" reasons but by the imperatives of belonging to the Center.

Since the days of the Resistance the central position of the MRP has been conditioned by its close bonds with the Socialist Party. The parochial school question seemed a dead issue from 1944 to 1951. The RPF deliberately revived the old quarrel when it introduced the Barrachin bill. The move was prompted by party politics much more than by a concern for education and justice. The MRP, falling into the trap, was pushed to the right, vacating a center where the Radicals triumphantly took over.

The MRP, born of the Resistance and representing its right, was led by temperament, and above all by historical vocation, into practicing what it believed were the ideas of General de Gaulle. Hence the relative intransigence of Georges Bidault's Indochinese policy. In the meantime, the RPF, pursuing relentlessly its move from extreme right toward center, made an about-face, condemning Georges Bidault's ill-fated policy and upholding the Indochinese peace proposals of Pierre Mendès-France.

This double play by the RPF forced the MRP rightward and widely opened the center to the thin ranks of the Radicals, who became the arbiters of power simply by virtue of the RPF's desire to be seated at their side.

The political power of the center is amazing. Within the Radical camp, henceforth center party *par excellence,* a slight displacement of popularity from right to left, from René Mayer to Pierre Mendès-France, is enough to create a strong displacement toward the left of the government's majority in the National Assembly. When the premiership passed from the hands of René Mayer to Pierre Mendès-France, the left wing of the government's supporting majority gained no less than 203 votes.

The internal divisions of this four-party Center assume a violent character because of the breadth of the political movements they cause. In February 1955 one could observe the following play on the French political stage: a Radical Prime Minister (Mendès-France) overthrown by a Radical deputy (René Mayer) only to be replaced by a new Radical Prime Minister (Edgar Faure). This maneuvering ended in a large shift of the government's majority toward the right, and the loss by the Left of 200 votes. Can a party survive such shocks? It presupposes an extraordinary elasticity. The inevitable scission of the Radical Party during the fall of 1955 brought about a sudden thinning of the Center's ranks: its right wing allied with the solid Right in order to spring the surprise election of January 1956. Behind the banner of Mendès-France its left wing allied with the Socialists for electoral purposes in order to found the Republican Front. After the election the real Center found itself limited to the UDSR and to the Social-Republicans, both of them weakened by serious electoral losses. This comparative void has reconfirmed the MRP in a central position which has suffered serious losses since 1951, thus bringing back to the French political mechanism its atmosphere of crisis: total Right versus total Left. The oscillations might very well have resulted in a Popular Front patterned on the 1936 style had it not been for a return to a MRP-Socialist alliance, reminiscent of the years 1946–1948, which might put through moderate yet assured social reforms if the world situation allows.

What about the influence of the world situation in the

near future? We cannot prognosticate, but we can point out the normal functioning of the French political mechanism: a worldwide weakening of liberal structures can start off serious oscillations (total Left–total Right), their strengthening can result in a return to government by the centers (Center Right versus Center Left).

Now government by the Center can take on unusual forms in France: the one prevalent during the period 1860–1870 or, more recently, the style peculiar to Pierre Mendès-France in 1954–1955. The latter's very personal style won him the support of voters inclining toward caesarism. This support, not very significant as yet, could swell to the point of creating a center reformist movement of the type the RPF might conceivably have promoted.

A few pages back we offered the notion of a hypothetical situation in which the RPF, accepting the French parliamentary regime, might have become its arbiter and the center party *par excellence.* The Social-Republicans, direct heirs of the RPF, were hard hit by the surprise election of January 1956, but at least they succeeded in shaking off their rightist elements and attained their goal, to sit beside the Radicals—better yet: to place themselves between the two sections of a Radical Party henceforth split into right and left factions.

An examination of the parliamentary quarrels of 1954–1955 convinces us that consciously or unconsciously the Social-Republicans strove to obtain this split between Radicals. They were successively for and against the Laniel government, for and against the Mendès-France government, for and then violently against the Edgar Faure government, for and against the single-member constituency, and for and against the policies followed in North Africa. By dissolving Parliament, the Center Right government of Edgar Faure attempted to push the RPF's electorate toward the right. This maneuver conformed strictly to British parliamentary procedure. But France is not Britain. Presenting themselves as a center party, the Social-Republicans abandoned their extreme right position, which the Poujade group occupied. Depending on the particular candidates, the Social-Republicans, during the campaign, at times joined forces with the Republican Front, at other times opposed it. In other words, they widened the breach between Radicals in the hope of replacing radicalism.

But that breach left a relative void in the center. The MRP, which the RPF intrigues of 1951 had forced rightward, took advantage of this void to renew its past alliance with the Socialists and help them secure power. From that point on the Social-Republicans aimed at destroying this rather fragile patchwork. Better even than the parochial school question, the Algerian problem seemed to lend itself to maneuvers fomenting dissension. After all, had not the Socialists and the MRP already clashed over Indochina? An agreement between Radicals and Social-Republicans that would have led to the recall of General de Gaulle did not seem excluded, and the hypothetical situation we imagined for 1951 could still have been realized.

Nevertheless, the Socialists and the MRP managed to stay united on the North African question as well as on European and social policy. Of course, there still remained economic and financial difficulties to be hurdled. For this reason Mendès-France astutely refused the portfolio of Minister of Economic Affairs; there was every reason to suppose that an inflationary crisis would in itself kill the alliance between the MRP and the Socialists. And French economic crises depend on world prices. The world situation governs the answer to a crucial question: Can the movement for capitalistic reform ally with labor to solve the problems confronting underdeveloped countries? Thus economic problems and problems of the French Union are but two faces of the same coin.

The international situation will decide which of three possibilities are to occur in France: a return to marked oscillation between total Right and total Left, a powerful strengthening of the Center, or a preservation of the present Center Left majority. By international situation, we mean an international economic and financial conjuncture based on development of the world societies of Asia, Africa, America, and Europe.

For France is bound both to the destiny of the Eurasiatic continent and to the destiny of continents overseas. We shall look at this more closely later. But a preliminary lesson must always be in our minds: the French government is in the tow of problems. And why? Because the Center, where government heads are recruited, manufactures a party for each type of problem and hence manufactures a government for each type of problem. The time necessary for that party and for that government to be constituted creates a situation in which the government achieves only what the most urgent circumstances impose.

In France governments do not pose problems. But problems do impose governments.

IX

The European Question

THE first effort of French industrialization bore on the districts surrounding the Massif Central. According to the economists of the period, 1830–1860, this region was destined to become a French Midlands. But apart from the fact that after 1850 newly equipped British districts somewhat lessened the Midlands' economic domination, France's first industrial center did not prove to be suited to heavy industry, that indispensable foundation of modern equipment.

After 1880 the situation changed. The coal fields in the North were at last being exploited and the iron deposits of Lorraine had been integrated into the cycle of steel production. The French position was steadily improving. Although France had little hope of matching England and Germany, her sources of energy no longer showed up as poorly as they had, say, in 1865, when the German potential, moving by vast strides, had definitely outstripped that of France.

The displacement of French industrial zones from the South toward the North and from the West toward the East underlines the fact that after 1880 France industrially was no more than a margin, an important margin, to be sure, but not the most important, of an industrial whole extending from England to Bohemia—a whole concentrating particularly in the north of Europe though stretching a minor branch to northern Italy. In any event, the heart of industrial Europe is not situated in France. The center of gravity is northeast of her.

But Europe is not exclusively industrial; it possesses vast zones that remain essentially agricultural. On each side of a Germany blessed by coal, two nations acutely experienced the vicissitudes of industrialization: France, close to the Atlantic, and Russia, whose difficulties were due less to the uncertainties of her subsoil than to her remoteness from the Atlantic and to her very immensity. For 150 years the agricultural countries undergoing a slow industrialization looked toward France—at least at those moments when the periodic explosions of Germany allowed them to do so. For the last twenty years these same countries have also been looking toward Russia, where, as soon as technical advancement was on a scale commensurate with the vastness of the Russian continent, industrial progress leaped forward, offering the world the example of the most rapid industrialization of an agrarian nation yet known.

One can, therefore, distinguish three Europes. The first, strictly industrial and Atlantic, has its maritime borders running from Le Havre to Hamburg; its heart lies near the Ruhr. This is the "Little Europe" which, as we have seen, stretches a narrow arm toward Milan and the Gulf of Genoa. The second, called "Great Europe," is basically the historical Europe, which, indeed, was rather conscious of its identity from 1860 to 1930. Until 1917 this Europe included Russia, which is undeniably the geographical and historical extension of eastern Europe. The third Europe is the one which, refusing the break of 1917, would be ready to embrace a more Asianized Russia.

Historically, the earliest-organized entity of this centrifugal complex was France itself. She was the first crucible in which races melted into a coherent nation. France underwent the bloody experience of the Albigensian crusade and of the wars of religion. Yet she pursued her national crystallization comparatively shielded from the wounds of the great schisms (such as the Oriental or the northern Protestant schism) and benefited from the enrichment brought by the Atlantic. All of this contributed to her predominance as the key nation of Europe during the seventeenth and eighteenth centuries, the one whose culture was the most coherent, the most attractive.

England profited too much from Atlantic trade not to accept a certain break with the continent. During the Middle Ages she abandoned her territorial ambitions in France; later, she severed relations in Hanover without undue regret.

Austria has had an amazing destiny. Master of the mountain passes barring the north-south and east-west routes, she was the imperial heir during four centuries. Then in the age of railroads and airplanes she had to resign herself to becoming a second Switzerland.

Germany has known the most tragic of destinies. The theater of pitiless wars of religions, it was the traditional field of battle lying between the Occidentals and the Slavs, between the Catholics from the South and West and the Protestants from the North. Thanks to its industrial potential, the Germany of the nineteenth century, excluded from the seas and belatedly formed as a nation, became the great center of European steel and by virtue of this the most redoubtable arsenal in the history of the world.

England, outside Europe proper, yet too close not to be concerned, tolerated France's efforts to surround Germany with a ring of alliances contracted with the smaller agrarian nations. These inevitable alliances were the nightmare of Bismarck. In the Germany of Wilhelm II and of Hindenburg they gave rise to an obsession of besiegement which converted toys into guns and a parliamentary regime into tyranny.

Can so many centuries of hostility be transformed into fraternal co-operation, or do they create an insurmountable obstacle? Can the reconciliation of Europe be achieved solely within Europe's own boundaries? Or must old hatreds be melted into a much larger group, Eurasia, for instance, which has a solid historical background and is a more representative world entity?

We cannot give even a rapid summary of the varied but uniformly fruitless efforts made by Europe to co-ordinate Europe. Nevertheless, we should take note that in the mid-nineteenth century technicians and capitalists hoped, with a faith inspired by the teachings of Saint-Simon, that industrial progress would bring nations into lasting harmony. In the 1900's, however, the conciliatory efforts of the great Franco-German capitalists ran afoul of nationalistic opinions which labor leaders themselves espoused in order better to denounce the "treason" of the business world.

The break between bosses and workmen helped maintain a widespread public suspicion of any private international enterprise covering the industrial markets of Europe. Before 1944, then, every effort at tearing down national barriers met with failure. The nationalization of power companies in France and the progress of socialization from 1944 to 1947 appeased labor's anxieties in regard to a European market, but it exacerbated those of private management, which has remained in possession of the French steel industry. And above all, the Americans, whose good intentions are matched by their lack of understanding of European psychologies, do not grasp the political difficulties inherent in the rapprochement of two peoples all the more different in that American credit encouraged the persistence of liberalism in Germany while it feigned ignorance of, but nevertheless tolerated, a strong margin of socialization in France. Despite the good will demonstrated by the French Socialists—a good will stemming in great part from their faith in technical progress—it is evident that the European Coal and Steel Community is a round table with very uneven legs. The financing of Germany's industry being an easier, a much easier, matter than the financing of France's industry, it required a solid dose of idealism for the French to accept the principle of free competition. Will this idealism be met by a corresponding generosity on Germany's part?

The tragedy is that, if German idealism is a deep and incontestable national trait, it does not manifest itself at the same time as does French idealism. In Germany it blossoms on the morrow of economic and military catastrophes—in other words, precisely when France's psychological positions are tightest and most unbending. When the worst of the crisis has spent itself, France relaxes; but by then, seized by the mechanical dizziness of her industrial power, Germany has resumed its positive, concrete way of life. Will the history of 1848, 1860, 1890, and 1919 repeat itself today?

In France the theoreticians of technical progress do not pay much attention to the psychological aspect of financial problems.

Among French technocrats Jean Monnet is the least sensitive to psychological factors. For him, the fervent promoter of European economic integration, money is money. Possessing none of the traits of a tribune, he neglects the fact that a people can be educated and he despairs of the Frenchman's financial education. In his view France is congenitally incapable of creating great capital. And wishing to protect capitalism from communistic experimentation, he can only conceive of an alliance with German, Scandinavian, or Anglo-Saxon capitalism. Furthermore, he rallies certain economic Malthusians to his views.

But those who criticize Jean Monnet do so with a disarming childishness. To state that "money can always be found" is absurd; it is verbosity characteristic of the very worst kind of Malthusians—the lazy ones. The financial education of a nation is possible, though not without serious effort.

Certainly, there is such a thing as a psychological technique. However, it is far from having the concrete efficiency of ordinary techniques; one can only turn to it after a thorough appraisal of the situation. Confidence is deserved, not ordered; in other words, it can be achieved for a whole whose individual parts have given reassuring proof of their soundness.

Now this whole has been achieved only partially by the establishment in "Little Europe" of Christian parties, covering traditionally Catholic territories, that have become the arbiters of political power. The situation would not change, even if we were to witness the simultaneous rise to power of the Socialist parties (see Figure 18). But should socialism develop in France while liberalism progresses across the Rhine, the divorce might express itself by a violent imbalance between French and German financing.

In the past German liberalism has not paved the way to a labor government of the British or French type. It has led to communistic or nationalistic extremes. Will things be different tomorrow? What do we know about the political psychology of the farmers of East Germany? If they pass from Russian occupation to a democratic republic, will they be converted to liberalism, to labor? Or will they once more dream of violent solutions? In any case the establishment of the European Coal and Steel Community (ECSC) is an act of faith in technique, in a technique which ignores the basic psychological environments. The wager may be good or bad, but a wager it is.

Because French industry is not so generously endowed by nature as Germany's, its prices are higher. The thriving fraction of French industry is obliged to participate heavily in the expenses that the nation has to bear because of its persistent rural elements and its commitments overseas. The French steel industry is particularly prosperous, but it cannot escape the laws of the nation. Either the German steel industry will show understanding, in other words, will help the French steel industry face its exterior burdens (in particular the agricultural development of the overseas territories), or else the French steel industry in order to survive will have to withdraw, partially at least, from the French economic complex. One can only hope that the advantages France may find in the new market will compensate for the loss resulting from a possible alienation of her steel industry. This also appears more like a wager than a calculation.

France's predicament in the ECSC reflects the old theoretical bent of the French mind, rarely positive even in technical matters.

But the drama that surrounded the European Defense Community is even more characteristic. German rearmament did not present itself to American public opinion as a moral rehabilitation but as an expedient to obtain manpower. In order to lessen the threat of an autonomous German rearmament, Christian and Socialist France proposed an integration of military forces. Such an integration would have been very costly for France, both in men and in equipment, but it might possibly have created a *psychological shock* of a new type. As wagers go, it offered more chances and more coherence than the steel wager, but it was not based on valid technical data; this explains the jamming of the French political mechanism in the face of the project. Paradoxically enough, this adventurous project provoked the hostility of the most adventurous elements of the Left and the Right. In the name of technique military technicians voiced their doubts as to the practicability of a composite army; their arguments had already been heard in 1938 in respect to the Czechoslovakian army. Caution and Malthusianism grew most anxiously articulate at the prospect of an effort that would oblige France to maintain two armies: one in Europe, a large new one overseas. In short, the composite character of the project incited a composite opposition of the Right and the Left. From then on, the French political machine's only aim was to make time by delaying German rearmament as long as feasible. America was becoming uneasy. In the meantime West Germany was thriving on disarmament; the resultant economy in means and manpower allowed it to devote all of its efforts to industry, notably to its steel industry. The drama ended in a brutal climax. The cosignatories of the treaty were given three days to accept modifications France had taken three years to formulate. A refusal ensued even though later France accepted German rearmament amid American acclamations.

Established on weak technical foundations, this immense project from a psychological viewpoint was undoubtedly the most completely European to have been born in France. Germany's good faith in regard to "Little Europe" is scarcely debatable. Western and southern Germany is essentially Catholic and industrial. Because of this, no dangerous inferiority complexes oppose it to Italy, France, or the Benelux. Its opening to the west might rid Germany of its old obsession of besiegement, of its complex of encirclement. The French problem is more grievous: for 150 years France has been torn between its role in Europe and its role overseas. Not so long ago Ferry clashed with Clemenceau, who refused to divert troops toward the colonies in order to hold Germany's arsenal in respect. Today France has been obliged to resign herself to the restoration of Germany.

The fact is that the Europe of 1950 is not so different from that of 1930. The only significant difference is that today Europe undergoes control by non-European nations. This may have the effect of guaranteeing peace on Europe's frontiers, but will it guarantee the creation of a real Europe?

The failures of a hastily assembled Little Europe do not necessarily imply the success of a Great Europe 1919 style, the most mythical of all. The transformations of the world act in a deeper manner: the development of a modern China and of a modern India will bring Russia back to the relatively Occidental position it held until 1917. Intelligently planned and efficiently applied, the Communist regime is the best suited to the rapid integration of industrial techniques in a society of the old rural type—whence communism's success in countries where technical transformations have not yet taken hold; whence its success in Slavic countries, in the Balkans, and perhaps in old rural eastern Germany. Is this Russian success the very reason which bars its march toward the west? It would be quite a paradox, but the psychology of nations, even of Cartesian nations, offers such paradoxes.

For much longer and with fewer resources France has also striven to implant industrialism in a rural country. She succeeded on her own metropolitan territory. And this success long made her the focus point of rural Europe. Can she hope for a comparable success in Africa? Would a failure signify the end of a great historical destiny?

Can the modernization of western Islam be accomplished by France alone, in the way that the modernization of Transcaucasian and Transcaspian Islam was by Russia alone? Will it be accomplished by Europe? Or by a world organized into a coherent pattern?

Undoubtedly, a careful psychological study of the problem would yield some elements of an answer. In its absence we shall perforce multiply question marks till life has pronounced a verdict. And yet life presents an open book. All we need to do is read. But who can read the preambles that life writes? Shall we always wait for the day of judgment? Learning how to read life is the first step in remedying Europe's vicissitudes. Unfortunately, the lessons of intellectual and moral reform which Renan drew from the war of 1870 were beyond the grasp of the nation's conscience. Russia is the fatherland of psychology, England of economic psychology. And France? There psychology has elected no domain; it belongs to everyone and to no one.

Let's consider a few of the failures in the historical attempt to unify Europe. First, Napoleon's failure. At the beginning of the industrial era he conquered an agrarian Europe, not by virtue of France's industrial power, but precisely because she had failed to convert herself into an industrial society. After 1870, as in 1914, why then did Germany fail? Because it succeeded too rapidly, too easily, in establishing a process of industrialization that could not be applied in any other European country. This failure was rife with tragedy: Goering's pre-1939 plan for economic expansion succeeded in large sectors of central Europe only because it was sustained by a conquering industry which was simultaneously building a military power that blew up in Germany's hands and ravaged Europe.

From 1860 to 1917 the economic destinies of France and of Russia were bound together, not for political reasons but for essentially human reasons. In both countries industrialization encountered the same sort of obstacles: difficulties of communication and of mobilization of rural manpower, inaccessibility of natural wealth. Similar sources of financing created a parallel development of technical progress.

Who will better succeed, France or Russia? Will success depend on their mutual agreement? And would such an agreement prove compelling enough to check German industry within Europe, while encouraging its expansion outside Europe? Furthermore, could such an agreement call forth the nonegoistic assistance of the older industrial powers? This is the crux of the European problem.

And how has the French government reacted to these problems? Statistically, French Africa offers peaceful outlets for German industrial power. But psychologically, France's old and, until recently, her quite legitimate industrial timidity has instilled in her a fear of German industrial vitality. To erase this complex can one count on the support of the Atlantic powers? In 1920 as in 1950 the British and the Americans showed far more willingness to come to the assistance of German industry, highly productive under a liberal regime, than to French industry, only productive normally under a semisocialized regime.

There remains the possibility of Russian support. This explains an apparent paradox—the fact that the RPF deputies, after having vigorously campaigned against the Communists, took up positions against Germany in favor of a rapprochement with Russia. Thus French nationalism has recovered its positions of 1880 and, ignoring the Socialist Party, allows itself to be applauded by the Communists.

There are two different ways of solving this contradiction: *immobilisme,* a profoundly political expression of French economic Malthusianism—an *immobilisme* which refuses any manner of integration with Germany or Russia and awaits for solutions that time will impose on a government that will have neither foreseen nor prepared for them; or, on the contrary, a massive effort of industrial expansion that will deliver France of its old industrial inferiority complex and allow her to compete calmly and on equal or superior terms with German or Russian production.

We shall return to this capital problem in our conclusion.

X

Drama Overseas

THE map of Africa, as those of America and Asia, shows that, apart from Algeria, which deserves separate study, the French colonial empire developed in the wake of England's. Because of a double vocation, Eurasian and maritime, France was not in a position to exert all of her energy overseas. From the eighteenth century on her preoccupation with Germany distracted her from America. While gaining Lorraine, she lost Canada. In the same manner Napoleon was led to sell Louisiana. On the other hand, after the loss of Alsace and Lorraine in 1871, the France of Jules Ferry tried to forget her sorrow by action overseas in Indochina and Africa.

The time and effort expended in the watch over Europe were just so much diversion from an activity to which England devoted every bit of energy.

But also the colonial attitude of France, her vocation, differed greatly from England's. England was a merchant making out balance sheets, a trader with an alert eye to profits. The coast of India being a more profitable investment than the interior, England stayed on the coast line, only moving inland as the probability of profits grew. For more than a century British India was controlled by a trade company. Inevitable after the establishment of railroads, the transition from a purely commercial policy to a more systematic territorial occupation stirred up serious trouble—in particular, the revolt of the Sepoys, which resulted in the disappearance of the company and in the creation of an empire. The fact remains that the mentality of the administration in India was characterized by psychological traits which two centuries of trading had deeply marked. When, two generations later, India had become too costly an investment, it was given up.

The French mentality is oriented differently. Certainly, we have no right to ignore the efforts of English missionaries or the evident generosity embodied in a Wilberforce. We are merely exaggerating differences in character to render them more salient; no doubt, the reader will be able to adjust things equitably.

In the French economy exchanges play a minor role. It is a hard economy to express in terms of accounting, above all in the nineteenth century. The value of a cargo load is easy to measure, but how can one appraise the value of peasant or spiritual work? France exported few merchants, but she exported missionaries (religious and lay), soldiers, and peasants. It would be arduous to state to what degree such exports are "profitable."

In France the discussion of overseas expansion is all the more heated because the two conceptions confronting each other are the peasants' and the intellectuals'. For the sake of brevity we call a "peasant" the modest Frenchman, whether farmer, artisan, or humble employee. This class of colonial settlers does not go overseas to make a fortune but simply to live a little more freely, a little better than in France. This settler does not create an easily recoverable capital. He takes roots in the new earth, becomes part of the local economy, binds himself to the destiny of the country that has received him. He cannot leave it without a heartbreak which has little to do with the small material interests he may have acquired. Having no mobile capital, the alternative is simple: ruin or war.

In the nineteenth century there is little doubt that the conquest and the possession of the Sahara, even of West Africa, represented a very mediocre financial advantage for France—an advantage quite out of proportion with the sum of efforts required. But those efforts themselves (military occupation, administration) are unappraisable and in truth France's only satisfaction is an intangible one—the pride of her world presence. Beside her peasants, France exports officers, doctors, teachers, and civil servants. She administers and educates the new lands as she would a French county. One cannot imagine a less racial policy; yet, assuredly, it is also antigeographical and uneconomical.

Even Algeria in 1830–1840 was a poor investment. In twenty years there were 100,000 dead—many in combat against the incessant menace of proud and rugged native warriors, but many more in the fertilization of a wretched soil made dangerous by swamp fevers. Clearly a bad initial investment, yet blood signs more durable property titles than do the disputes of traders. This seems the first trait of French expansion.

The second is that manner of generously sowing the ideas of liberty and fraternity, of the rights of peoples, of respect for science and progress. Ideas belonging to the same race of peasants and artisans, but broadcast by a different social category less sensitive to the roots created by the patient labor of the seasons and the years.

Ideas, nevertheless, which are all the more effective that they contrast with British mercantilism. The huge size of Britain's commercial fortune and the reactions it provoked everywhere, and especially in Asia, made France stand out as the nation of ideals and disinterestedness. She often appeared as a power, a distant one to be sure, but at least one counteracting British expansion. Hence the relative favor she enjoyed and which prepared the way for her missionaries, her professors, and also her diplomats. It was esteemed preferable to fall under the French diplomatic and cultural system, even under the title *Protectorate* —today judged humiliating but in the nineteenth century considered a reassurance—than to become a commodity handled by a trade company.

This double character of French expansion, so different from British expansion whose trace it really followed, made France's success. She succeeded all the better in that her expansion embodied a fundamental French trait, poverty with great ideas.

One must add that the cult of laicism does not prevail outside metropolitan France. France respects Islam more than it does Roman Catholicism. And this with the consent of the French Christians themselves. For those who profess a militant laicism, the act of respecting Islam seems a fine way of obstructing the Roman Church. For the Christians, to respect Islam is to defend religion. In any event, Islam makes out quite well. Unfortunately, the education given by Islam in its mosque schools (distributing diplomas fairly generously to attract more students) is distressingly archaic despite recent and still very insufficient efforts—an education made fanatic because of its very inefficiency. One can scarcely imagine it able to tame the rugged African nature.

Let us glance at Africa. Its soil and its climate make it the hardest continent in the world to exploit. It has scarcely been touched by modern techniques. Africa's resistance to rational exploitation explains its long total neglect by the industrial and commercial powers of Europe (apart from a few territories in the South and bits of coast line in the East and in the West). There lay an ideal domain for French "vanity."

And an admirable vanity it is which builds hospitals and schools, which exports the Rights of Man and imports wood and peanuts, which sends to Africa a few adventuresome spirits and welcomes into French intellectual and political society African minds of great merit. France keeps an Africa which no one wanted. She will keep it so long as its commercial exploitation appears improbable. What will happen when this exploitation offers innumerable prospects and possibilities of success? Can a weak industry and a financial power narrow for want of education satisfy all the undertakings made possible, and hence rapidly inevitable, in a system of international competition? This is one of the most urgent tasks facing French modernization, one of the gravest problems facing Europe, or the Europes, one of the most vital tests confronting world collaboration.

The Anglo-Saxons succeeded in establishing important white settlements in several regions of the world: South Africa, Australia, Canada. As we saw, this was accomplished by reliance on the best available technical equipment—and, in any event, in regions where this equipment could offer profitable returns. As technical progress developed, these profit-bearing zones widened. Here a problem occurs: none of these zones was *absolutely* empty, and so the native population was slowly, methodically driven back.

The Frenchmen who expatriated went overseas with rudimentary equipment, not drastically different in nature from that used by the indigenous population—whence the numerous contacts with the natives, creating an understanding characteristic of French occupation; and France is proud of sharing this virtue with the Portuguese of South America. Crossbreeding between races is rendered easier, a greater harmony between occupant and occupied is the rule. This policy is at opposite poles from the Anglo-Saxon method of systematically driving back the natives and penning them in "reservations."

It is not that France has never practiced racial segregation. She did so at least once—from 1850 to 1870 in Algeria. Napoleon III had then inaugurated the so-called Arab Kingdom policy: the native population was isolated from the Europeans, each race was taught to move in its own zone, and separate administrations were set up. Napoleon III, as Arab sultan, governed the Algerians through "Arab Offices" headed by a Ministry of Algeria; to the French-born Algerians he was the Emperor. The two societies were arbitrarily separated by harshly traced frontiers; no mixing was to be tolerated. The French settlers vehemently protested against a state of affairs which limited their expansion; and in truth the number of Europeans did not increase. Their failure to increase was accented by the fact that, under the impulsion of the chimeric sultan Napoleon, the Arab Offices practiced a policy which purported to be generous and disinterested —in a word, pro-Arab. But the curious side to this experiment is that the native population did not increase either.

It seemed struck by sterility, as were the natives impounded in Anglo-Saxon "reservations."

In 1871 the Arab Offices were suppressed; the government put an end to the short-lived policy of systematic segregation. The French population increased rapidly and, in many respects, the native population even faster. The strength of France lay in this combination.

Yes, strength, if one considers the remarkable loyalty the Arabs have showed France until our day—a loyalty proved in the cruel tests of 1914-1918 and 1939-1945; a loyalty contrasting markedly with Britain's old troubles in Egypt. This was true in spite of the fact that Britain was always in a better position to assist Egypt economically than France was to aid Algeria.

But yesterday's strength is today's weakness. For now France, with a relatively limited technical equipment, must face the enormous problem created by a population of nine million. This mass, in its majority illiterate and consequently uninformed as to the possibilities actually offered by technical progress (which, moreover, has given rather piteous results in most of Islam), has been lured away by foreign radio propaganda. Undoubtedly, it overestimates the effect of industrial miracles. Attributing its stagnation to French occupation, it has rediscovered its old warlike atavism and the pride of freedom.

France, then, is in a strange position. From France herself—we insist on this point—two different currents have never stopped flowing. The one, intellectual, is inspired by generous theories; it encourages every aspiration to liberty, right, or nationalistic honor. And many of the nationalist Arab leaders were educated by France. The other current, made up of humble emigrants, has created a population of small and modest settlers: farmers, artisans, government employees. To the natives in general, these are the incarnation of arbitrary occupation, even though on the local, individual plane excellent relationships have been established between races and religions.

Obviously, France has also exported large-scale capitalistic enterprises, but in a smaller proportion than has England. The virtues of this overseas capitalism is that of being relatively mobile and capable of migrating from uncertain zones to more secure ones. And it is not this capitalism which has created the most painful problems in North Africa; it has not been a major stumbling block between European and natives; for, thanks to its mobility, big business adapts itself to every type of political situation.

The North African Frenchmen who belong to the modest classes cling to their property rights all the more tenaciously since their property is small, consisting of real estate rather than movable personal property. These Frenchmen are firmly attached to an administrative, juridical, and political form which, in their eyes, is their only secure protection. And in fact, their small holdings would very probably be unable to survive the shock of a profound political or legal transformation. In their anxiety the Frenchmen of North Africa have recovered that old insurrectional temperament which swept France at every revolution during the nineteenth century when the difficulties encountered by industrialization hit small property owners much harder than it did the wealthier classes.

This explains why the Franco-Tunisian negotiations demonstrated a greater preoccupation with administrative and juridical matters than with purely political matters. Each possible case had to be examined, and a veritable code was elaborated. A general declaration, touching only on the major political issues mutually agreed to, would undoubtedly have been preferable. In reality, the position of the small French property owners made it impossible. France's presence was more conspicuously capitalistic in Morocco, a far wealthier country than Tunisia, because it was colonized at a later date. In Morocco the French government found it much easier than it had in Tunisia to satisfy all elements by a general political declaration.

It is this intimate character of the Franco-Arab symbiosis which renders more excruciating the present revision of France's position in North Africa. There is no simple way out. France is refused the classic British expedient of a rapid and total evacuation.

In the face of these dramatic events the positions assumed by the various parties and governments evince a disarming type of determinism. The extreme Right defends occupation in the old military manner characteristic of the peasant soldier and of the soldier-artisan. The Center Right defends a British type of supple capitalism ready to adapt to any situation but also too fragile to operate alone. The extreme Left is quite satisfied to do nothing but continue exporting its ideologies. The Center Left hesitates between a purely ideological position and the defense of the little Frenchman and of his administration. The various Centers choose this or that program as events push one of their own members to power.

Still, the fundamental problem remains: Can Africa organize itself rapidly into valid industrial units? Can Tunisia and Morocco on the one hand, Algeria on the other, achieve this without assistance from outside? Can France alone bring the necessary help? The questions were the same in regard to Europe. Upon their answer depends the distant future of North Africa and the character of the grievous phases of transition which presently oppose, not so much the misery of the Arabs to the wealth of the French, but rather the underequipped Franco-Arab community to the various plans aimed at remedying this state of underequipment.

In any case it is not only France's territories in Algeria and her friends in Tunisia, Morocco, Africa, or Indochina, it is the totality of underdeveloped nations in the world who, still treasuring the memory of the great liberalism of French ideas, would be ready to welcome French technicians, French educators, and French equipment and would prefer a French modernity to Anglo-Saxon business.

Also, it is exactly that type of men, that type of equipment, that France lacks most. Not finding enough to meet her own Metropolitan needs, how could she find them for overseas? Basically, it is a problem of education more than of technology. Education is at the heart of every major problem confronting France.

French education is deficient. The army, which ought to be a civic and technical school, gets very little from the good will of recruits, who lose confidence for having hoped too much.

It was much easier to conquer an empire in 1880 than it is to organize one in 1950. To proclaim, as people do only too easily, that young Frenchmen are on the decline by comparison with their glorious elders is to utter a manifest countertruth. Doubtless they are as brave; and why not? They work harder—the youth of the whole modern world has undertaken heavier tasks than its elders—and, above all, they are more exacting. They have learned the limitations of heroism and the efficiency of techniques. They hunger for technique. No wonder they are deceived, at times disenchanted, to observe that school and army treat them as their elders were treated, in obsolete ways.

France needs an army of technicians and educators. She only has an army of soldiers. Yet it is not the soldiers' fault.

Historical evolution has differed for each people, for each group of peoples. But there is only one human fate, one mission for humanity. If you turn to the past, regretting without understanding, it is hard to rid yourself of the feeling of inequality between races. If you study the past to discover your future, that feeling becomes the most obsolete imaginable.

Yesterday heroism and war were the surest paths to glory. The acceleration of technical progress has defined the greatness of men and peoples in other terms. The new great nations of the twentieth century have conquered more by techniques than by war. Is France yesterday's nation or tomorrow's?

XI

Education at a Standstill

THE French university system is a century and a half old; it has changed little since Napoleon Bonaparte created it. Its past successes have consolidated its defects. A rigid structure, it can only be modified by a general reform; it stands no chance of undergoing a gradual evolution of the Anglo-Saxon variety.

In the last twenty years committees for educational reform, projects, bills, have amassed their dusty reams to no avail.

In the mid-twentieth century there are voices reassuring us that France owes her spiritual objectivity, her cosmopolitanism, to the study of Greek and Latin! As if China, India, and Iran did not also owe much to Greek and Latin. The only subject that really impassions political debates on education is that of religious education. Whichever the point of view, this amounts to dragging before the nation problems appropriate to the Constituent Assembly of 1789.

Clearly, a country producing 42 million kilowatt-hours of electricity needs men differently equipped and trained from those of a country with a production of less than 10 million kilowatt-hours (France in 1920), or of only a few hundred thousand kilowatt-hours (France in 1820).

Energy development in France came late by comparison with England and Germany. In common with most aspects of industrialization in France the effort to develop power is extremely intensive during periods of peace, this trait being more characteristic of Russia and of new nations than of countries that have already secured a certain potential. The effort is intensive because it must rapidly compensate for the long severe periods of stoppage created by crises and wars. Finally, the effort is more productive as we draw away from the period when coal reigned supreme over all phases of industry. As power moves away from its dependence on coal, France, a poor producer of coal, gains new possibilities.

We have purposely combined the topics of equipment and education. In reality, for certain highly concentrated industries—steel and chemical products—the eminent qualities of a small elite composed of French engineers and scientists succeed in meeting urgent technical problems: great dams, progress in traction, airplane prototypes, modern rolling mills. Fifteen thousand highly qualified technicians easily command great masses of workmen.

But concerns showing a high degree of technical concentration can work with stability and security only in a country whose *totality* offers a certain technical solidity. We have no room here to present in detail the numerous technical deficiencies that cause bottlenecks in French productivity. We shall simply mention a general phenomenon: the financing required by gigantic modern industries cannot depend on the small group of their managers; it must derive its strength from the national collectivity. For French finances to be coherent, then, the entire collectivity must have reached a high degree of modernization. At this point, education rises as an urgent problem.

EDUCATION AT A STANDSTILL

We cannot underestimate the prodigious success of communism in Russia. If the Americans succeeded in launching an industrialization of exceptional strength, they did so supported by an educated population coming from Europe. By 1920 the Americans were completely modernized. Russia's problem was vastly more difficult—to introduce the last word in technique into a relatively immobile population rooted in secular traditions and presenting no trace of modernity. All that we know leads us to believe that Russian communism discovered an effective solution.

At what price? We shall let the Americans calculate it, the Americans who, around 1900, labored under no weighty past and who relied as much, if not more, than the Russians did on European credit and techniques. France shall settle this debate only if she first resolves her own problems.

Her dilemma is precisely the following: French technical equipment, though inadequate, is in certain key sectors (power and heavy industry) decidedly advanced. But the nation's education prolongs into the heart of the twentieth century traditions all the more tenacious that they stem from a glorious past; it is an education in a cosmopolitan style just as reminiscent of the Middle Ages as of the 1900's.

When referring to the nation's education, we are not pointing solely at the university system, but just as much at the army, the press, the radio, the moral tradition, the education of the street both in terms of urban settings and of human behavior, the education of workshops and fields, of stores and offices. All of this constitutes a French educational heritage that has fallen behind the nation's technical equipment. The gap between the two appears the more striking that techniques prosper in certain privileged sectors.

The gap between a powerful motor and a heavy-footed

education is more serious still if, as the law invites us to do, we count as members of the national community millions of Algerians and millions of Frenchmen of all races overseas. Viewed in this vast perspective, is the French structure closer to the Russian or to the Anglo-Saxon type? If closer to the Russian type, can France hope to introduce modernity by another system than communism?

The whole matter leads to the following: Can French education, in the larger sense of the word, achieve from Flanders to the Congo that relative unity of behavior required for the cohesive maintenance of the whole—a cohesion, and we insist on the point, all the more difficult to attain since the gap is wide between the most and the least educated? Would the relative unity of education, the cohesion of the population, be more easily attained by relinquishing equatorial Africa? Or North Africa? We believe that if France is able to educate herself—with so many of her own citizens centuries behind—she will succeed in educating Africa.

In reality, no one has the power to decide whether France will be "cut off" at the Mediterranean or at the Sahara. Historical evolution will draw the "natural" frontiers of France in terms of her educational effort.

But everyone has the power, and therefore the duty, to contribute to the promotion of an education equal to the needs of the nation—an education embracing in a solidly conceived system, in a single cohesion of faith, hope, and charity, the greatest possible number of Frenchmen.

Conceived in these terms, French education must contend with two fundamental problems: the mass production of competent technicians and the mass production of leaders competent to solve the psychological and social problems (and hence the capital investment which is the concrete expression of the trust a people has in itself) created by the existence of an industry capable of inventing the world's finest models within the framework of a society that runs the gamut from extreme archaism to extreme modernity.

The vastness of the problem delays solution. Perhaps one might prefer a general solution occurring late so that it may be the more complete, the more rapidly effective. A delay can only be justified for that reason; the later the educational reform, the "deeper" it will go. To elude that reform possibly amounts to submitting to revolutionary events.

The objectives of French education are openly paradoxical. From the age of twelve, it patiently trains a very small elite with exceptional intellectual gifts while it abandons to chance the training of the middle and lower ranks of its future qualified personnel, for which, nevertheless, the demand is enormous. And it has not yet integrated the mass of peasants and artisans, who remain technically undereducated.

Such an educational system prevents France from understanding the ardor of underdeveloped countries intent on forming innumerable technicians in a matter of months. When they call on her help, they are immediately demoralized by her slow, drawn-out, punctilious system. In 1946, for instance, India was completely discouraged by the awesome requirements of the Ecole Polytechnique. North Africans and Frenchmen are in great need of accelerated training of the American or Russian pattern. Will the need finally be heard?

And what is the army waiting for before becoming a completely professional army, or rather, an army of professions? In Africa, particularly, it could prove an invaluable accelerated training center for qualified native personnel.

While creating too perfect an elite, France abandons the undereducated mass. From this fact spring imbalance and violent crises. Born of the Revolution and of the Empire, this education has led to economic Malthusianism, revolutions, and dictatorship. Each time she was forced into crisis during the twentieth century, France recovered, with a certain taste for swagger and grandiloquence, her love of action—even violent, heroic, costly action. Each time she recovered a certain energy, brutally marking popular psychology with new ideas that jelled into myths taken to be the gospel truth as soon as the crisis waned.

Actually, the wars and revolutions of France, so terribly costly on the economic plane, were grandiose and bloody schools. Will France be able to build schools of peace and progressive evolution as efficient as were the old schools of combat and destruction?

Powerfully assisted by new educational techniques, will France discover solutions differing from the violent ones practiced in the nineteenth century and during the recent wars?

This question brings our brief historical essays to a close. We reserve our conclusions in order to formulate them in the light of a few prognostications made possible by the positive sciences. But with due regard to local variations, these prognostications can only be interpreted within the perspective of the world's evolution.

PART THREE

*France's Destiny
the World's Destiny*

XII

France, the World's Crossroads

IN Europe's heyday the slightest English economic crisis had repercussions the world over, and any economic incident, however distant it might be, affected England's economic seismograph. In the political domain this sensitivity was a French prerogative. Not a single noteworthy political event occurred in France without circling the globe; but also, every political event occurring in the world modified French political structures in a more or less perceptible manner.

It is common knowledge that the birth of the French Communist Party within the French Socialist Party was directly linked to the success of the revolution that established the dictatorship of the proletariat in Russia. Simple and obvious as it may be, this phenomenon is only one of the latest in a series of adoptions by the French of foreign political phenomena.

The French Socialist party, called SFIO (Section Française de l'Internationale Ouvrière), intended by its very title to underline its international character. The First International was born in London with Karl Marx as the moving spirit. Afterward the French workingmen's party went through the painful splits experienced by all such parties in Europe. In 1905, finally, Jaurès responded to the Second International's pressures in favor of the unity of the French Socialists. French socialism has never ceased sharing the hopes and the trials of an international socialism whose character is essentially North European.

In fact, this international affinity is not the exclusive privilege of leftist parties. Conscious of their solidarity in all of Christian Europe—particularly in Lotharingian Europe, with ramifications in Latin America—Christian parties have developed; in France they are represented by the MRP.

Other political formations of the Right, because more ancient in origin, are more difficult to define and delimit. In any case, international political communities are not an exclusive privilege of the Left. The great landed interests have obtained political representation in all the capitalistic democracies. They are one of the mainstays of the British conservatives and of the Right in Germany, in Italy, and in the United States. Until recently they dominated the history of central European countries. Since the food market never demonstrates much elasticity despite the world's immense zones of undernourished populations, it follows that the defense of agrarian interests means protectionism and nationalism. It is the substitution of the label "program" for that of "class consciousness" which masks the cosmopolitan nature of the rightest agrarian parties.

Small rural property subsists with greater vitality in France than elsewhere. It escaped the feudalism characteristic of the Balkans and it is more widely representative than in England or Germany. Politically, small property walks willingly in the footsteps of the French agrarian parties. But, as in certain Nordic countries, it shows no repugnance toward a certain type of socialism justified by small property's constant reliance on the state for firm market prices. As a case in point, the originality of the position adopted by winegrowing districts is peculiarly French because of the magnitude of the wine industry in France. The numerous small winegrowers have slid toward socialism by virtue of their constant appeals for state support. The French rural structure contributes significantly to this sort of unbalanced swinging from conservatism to socialism, thus adapting the dual British system to France.

Industrial life has approximately the same fate. More than in any country of the world, with the possible exception of Latin America, the beginnings of industrialization are connected with great landed property—hence that union of industrial and agrarian interests which has dominated the French Right. "Orleanism" grew out of the conversion of this double aristocracy which renounced monarchical obedience to espouse a parliamentary regime as a source of political stability. For that reason, the struggle between conservatives and liberals never took hold in political life as it did in Britain. There the interests of capitalistic land property and those of capitalistic industry were at odds. Practically the same condition prevailed in Germany. In France they combined. As a result the political pendulum swinging from country to city never inspirited French political life as it did England's. In the twentieth century, however, with the end of the British Liberal Party, the pendulum started moving between Conservatives (agrarian and industrial) and Labour, so that the present British scene has more points in common with the French situation than it previously did.

French parliamentarianism in the nineteenth century,

not having the ample, all-inclusive character of Britain's, tolerated the survival of numerous nonparliamentary traditions, which at times transformed into antiparliamentary tendencies—traditions and tendencies which have moved intact into the twentieth century.

We can, in fact, observe a curious contrast. While the conservative-socialist dualism is doubtless more natural to France than to Britain, it functioned much sooner in Britain. In England, indeed, Labour very naturally took over the Liberals' role as champion of urban interests at the very moment when in the cities the political vocation of the masses was gaining strength against management. But in either case the background is the same, the city. Classic liberalism divided between conservatism, which it rejuvenated, and Labour. In France the nineteenth century did little to prepare a dialogue between city and country. And the dialogue between those whom we call the "Orleanists" and the Socialists never took place. The former alone embodied the parliamentary regime. The latter embodied the opposition to the regime. The prospect of socialism's coming to power was viewed as a revolution; hence its late, costly, and uneasy accession as moving spirit of the Popular Front in 1936. Even after the integration of socialism with parliamentary government, the Right and the Left felt uncomfortable about it all.

This uneasiness fostered nonparliamentary political forms. Communism was their expression on the left. On the right the refusal to accept socialism hid under the mask of antirevolutionary loyalism. And the extreme Right continued to agitate the question long after socialism had proved, as the Labour Party had in Britain, that it fully respected the rules of the parliamentary game.

From then on agitation by the Right stood out more

directly as a form of antiparliamentarianism. Is the phenomenon peculiar to France? Certainly not. It can take on two different aspects. In central and eastern Europe the tardiness of industrialization brought about brutal reactions: industrial explosions in the Germany of Bismarck and Hitler, in the Russia of Stalin. French cities have at times known such impulses of revolt against the parliamentary regime, impulses favorable to authoritarian regimes. In certain respects the popularity of General Boulanger belongs to this category, as well as the stiffening of the Radicals under the leadership of Pierre Mendès-France in 1953 and, of course, the wave of urban discontent kindled by the RPF in 1947 and 1951.

Rural France, particularly in the West and South, offers examples of a rightist agitation less intent on hastening industrialization than on safeguarding the nation's peasant and artisan understructure. The most characteristic example is offered by the Poujade movement in 1956—and, not so long ago, by the monarchists of the Action Française.

This phenomenon develops out of the relative slowness of French urbanization and industrialization. Furthermore, its manifestations are observable in every technically underequipped country: Latin America, Asia, the Near East. There, as in France, extreme rightist agitation awakens monarchical, feudal, and religious loyalties, while waving the banner of integral nationalism.

Mediterraneans, the French react as do other nations along the shores of the Mediterranean. Having lived under the absolute monarchy of the Bourbons, the French react as have numerous peoples whose historical destiny unrolled close to theirs.

For such is the curious political destiny of France: socialism in Europe, socialism in France; communism in Russia, communism in France; parliamentarianism in Britain, parliamentarianism in France; monarchical reactions in Latin countries, monarchical reactions in France.

Until now we have shown what France owes to the world, or what links France to the rest of the world. What new elements does France bring to the world? Her strongest, most original contribution is to have remained a pilot nation combining with an unmatched synthetic power the totality of the world's political tendencies. This, of course, is somewhat true of all continental European nations, but somewhat only, for France—and the smaller neighboring nations that more or less share her political ideas—have not really known the great catastrophes of fascism and Hitlerism: she was their victim, not their agent. France endured a Franco type of regime (Vichy), but for a short time only in the throes of military defeat. In short, the French regime is, par excellence, one which has achieved very complex yet almost balanced political syntheses.

This relative equilibrium, maintained within a structure that accommodates every contradiction, is a lively subject of interest to every nation desirous of directing its political progress along a median road.

Are we justified in using the word "desirous"? To a great extent the conditions of existence of those nations rule their regime. The coincidence between types of political regimes and living standards is too obvious a fact not to be at least briefly mentioned.

There again France stands on middle ground. Doubtless Metropolitan France is not in direct physical contact with nations having low living standards. But through its Algerian departments, through Africa, it controls a good part of the countries which in modern international jargon are termed "underdeveloped."

Through her Mediterranean border France belongs to that group of Mediterranean countries so original in their economic and social structure and with low living standards, but progressing perceptibly by comparison with old Asia or with the heart of Africa.

Through her eastern frontier France is bound to nations enjoying a relatively high living standard.

Through her maritime and continental frontiers to the north France shares the high living standards of Britain and Belgium.

Our summary description might convey the notion that the different French living standards are geographically distributed. This would be a gross exaggeration. In reality, these different living standards occur in a narrow imbrication that spreads throughout France. And though possessing no common frontier with the proletarian dictatorships, France contains several regions—notably, Berry— where the problem of modernizing, industrializing, and raising living standards presents itself in terms resembling those of prerevolutionary Russia: entrenched rural routines, weak capitalistic credit, and uncertainty of an industry confronted by the Anglo-Saxon type of economic competition. Thus, if at times French communism appears to be the organic extension of the popular democracies projecting right into the heart of Europe, it also answers the natural aspirations of districts of ill-defined structure in the interior of France. This sort of imbalance threatens all of France's mountain frontiers.

Such considerations are far from applying only to communism. It can be said that many French *départements* offer every conceivable trait, each one of which can be related to a particular region of the globe. As in a microcosm France reproduces humanity's problems. This is a significant aspect of France. We shall come back to it later.

It is a fascinating and fertile study to measure to what extent Paris is not a region of France with localized political and economic reactions. Yet all French phenomena extend to Paris and intersect one another there. Nowhere else is a capital more truly a capital. No city shows as cosmopolitan a balance. No doubt because of their commercial principles Anglo-Saxon cities have a better representation of Far Eastern peoples (yet Paris has many Indochinese); but they do not adopt the moral or industrial structures of the Orient and in any case they exclude Slavic structures, which Paris does not.

This study is too succinct to close the debate on the world character of France and of her capital. Moreover, it is not impossible that France and Paris are in a process of regionalization, while New York and the United States, so regional only fifty years ago, are in a process of internationalization.

But at least this study will suffice, we hope, to suggest how vain it is to criticize thoughtlessly the obvious vices of the French political regime. In truth no country is so difficult to govern. This is the price France must pay for the privilege of being so broadly international—of being a juxtaposition of diverse societies opposed yet united within one nation; a juxtaposition of political attitudes, exclusive elsewhere, which here blend into a single regime.

XIII

The Advance of Progress: The North Atlantic

TECHNICAL progress is the axis of the modern world. This became true toward the middle of the eighteenth century. Capital is a show of confidence, of certainty, of freedom of action, and of ever more abundant riches placed at the disposal of a few privileged beings, so that they can upset and renovate technical equipment and societies and renew the tools of production according to the inspiration of scientists, inventors, and clever jacks-of-all-trades. Until the mid-twentieth century only a few western political thinkers had realized that this perpetual rejuvenation and development of equipment could be accomplished by the state: it had always been considered the exclusive domain of enterprising individuals. Previously, it was thought that the state's only duty was to observe and enforce a strict laissez-faire policy, giving free reins to the "peaceful" rivalries of fiery businessmen. The game of competition was then based on the absence of rules, emulation leading to the victory of the best. While contemplating this "loyal" battle, Darwin, a great reader of Malthus and of the economists of his time, discovered the nucleus of his famous evolutionary theory. From that time on economic competition appeared to be a mere extension of nature's competition. We should not be surprised that at the end of the nineteenth century most politicians considered capitalistic liberalism a natural phenomenon. The unwise intervention of the state, the insertion of any regulation prompted by noneconomic considerations, was viewed as a dangerous threat to the laws of nature and hence as an intrusion that would slow down progress or conjure "monsters" harmful to humanity's harmonious development.

The relative ease with which England could tap supplies of raw materials with her abundant coal easily mined and ships that could penetrate inland thanks to estuaries and tides—all of this rapidly carried Britain to the forefront of progress in Europe. By the eighteenth century Voltaire was praising in verse and in prose the modernity of an England advancing impetuously along the roads of mechanical progress and free commercial competition.

More than British thought, French thought (and particularly French biology) was absorbed by the problem of adaptation to environment. It so happens that France's physical environment does not lend itself as well as England's to technical progress. Assuredly, France does not lack coast lines, but its seas rarely penetrate inland. The Rhone is difficult to ascend, and, in any case, the Mediterranean has become no more than an annex of the Atlantic. The Garonne is a rather good navigable river; unfortunately, it crosses a country without an industrial subsoil. The Seine meanders endlessly. The Loire is obstructed by innumerable sand bars. In short, from the eighteenth century to our day all French businessmen have complained of the high cost and the difficulty of transportation. As a result, French products are expensive, and though the progressive spirits of yesterday's France admired England, they also feared it. Or, rather, they admired it when they were theoreticians; they feared it when they were businessmen. This is but another phase of the divorce between thought and action.

This preliminary observation explains why Nantes, Bordeaux, Le Havre, Boulogne, Dunkerque, and even Lyons and Marseilles are more readily Anglophile than industrial communities in central France such as Bourges, Montluçon, or Guéret. In the first group a certain harmony exists between theory and practice; elsewhere theory and practice are at odds.

Problems of transportation are not the only obstacles. In France coal is a source of misery. There are small coal deposits around the Massif Central; they are easy to mine but are of no consequence. In the North there are relatively abundant coal deposits; but they lie deep and are hard to reach. The first great French coal-mining companies underwent losses and failures. French coal production really started rising more than a century after England's; the gap between the two productions has never been bridged. On the other hand, France is rich in iron, richer even than England, but the quality of her ore is sometimes wanting; hence France's tardiness in achieving a profitable exploitation, but hence also the comparative ease with which she can make up lost time. There exist, then, two different aspects of heavy French industry, in fact two different Frances: an iron-ore France rather more favored than England, a coal France far less favored than England—particularly in the southern half of the country (see Figure 2).

Consequently, until the twentieth century the French industrial structure has always been behind that of Britain, and the British type of economic psychology has never spread uniformly throughout France. Certain regions are more readily receptive than others: especially, Normandy (iron centers and ports), Lorraine and, with certain reservations, the North (also a few isolated pockets—Lyons, Saint-Etienne, Marseilles, Bordeaux). Since political inclinations tend to follow economic inclinations, a great part of France has never adopted the modes of thought and action, or the governmental conceptions, characteristic of England.

To judge properly what regions are open or closed to a certain sympathy for British institutions and practices it would be necessary to take stock of activities which, until the twentieth century, have played a more important role in France than industry. Technical progress in England appeared first under the form of agricultural progress. Tools, fertilizers, the selection of plants and breeding stocks, and the rotation of crops soon proved the usefulness, indeed, the profits, to be derived from regrouping property into large farming estates. Yields became truly competitive only on farms of more than one hundred acres. Starting with the eighteenth century, England waged war against the little landholders to fatten the larger ones. France, seized by the enthusiasm of her agricultural theoreticians, of her physiocrats and other philosophers of nature, tried to do the same. But again, the zones where the British system could penetrate most readily were far from extending through all of France. In the region of Paris, in the plains of Picardy, in the East, things went along rather easily, helped by an already specialized structure that favored the modernization of average and large farms. Flanders resisted this movement, as did the greater part of the South, where small, very small, farms have subsisted undaunted. Thanks to Marc Bloch's studies we know that Brittany must also be tied to this medieval agricultural structure. Practically then, two-thirds of France remain to this day faithful to a pre-English type of agrarian economy.

Now, views on property rightly depend on whether tenure does or does not lend itself to the British type of land reform. Modernly equipped farms profiting from high technical yields could, if absolutely necessary, enter into a competitive liberal regime. We say "if absolutely necessary," for until the middle of the nineteenth century landowners demanded rather high protective tariffs. They had to recover the expense of the long transformations and modernizations of their farms. Later the yields of British agriculture, and the capital it had accumulated, allowed it to assume the liabilities inherent in the integral liberalism which, for nearly a century, was to remain the golden rule of British economy. To be sure, the right to property was sacred, but landowners enjoyed no other privileges.

In France it is quite another picture. The majority of farms were unable to acquire modern equipment, the yields remained low, the prices uncompetitive. In the nineteenth and twentieth centuries the farmer on his small land —too small to sustain modernization—needed and demanded protection. For him the state cannot be the liberal British state; it must be the protective state; it must remain the protective state it had already been for centuries under the monarchy. Certainly, the right to property is dear to the French peasant's heart. His ties to the earth are ancient, quite anterior to the Civil Code, and the word "property" covers with a new term an old psychological reality. In any event, property cannot, as in England, convey the idea of complete freedom: it is too burdened by debts. The peasant expects of the state, of the state's protection, that he be given the means to eke a livelihood out of his labor. More subject than citizen, the rural Frenchman continues to expect sustenance from his sovereign.

These considerations allow us to delineate the zones where a psychology based on economic liberalism has some chance of flourishing. Of course, even in regions where this mentality thrives, the assimilation is not complete. It is impossible to protect French metallurgy because of its poverty in coal while exposing it to free international competition because of its wealth in iron. It is impossible to protect the wheat of small farms while handing over to free international competition the wheat grown on large estates.

Consequently, the profit-making French farmer or industrialist really enjoys a double advantage: he has both advantages of modern equipment and high yields on the English style while profiting by state protection on the French style. The great landholders and the great French industrialists have two trumps in hand. They are blessed by freedom (capitalistic property) and sheltered from the perils of freedom. Tradition has converted this practice into a right.

We hope this will explain why, though it found zones well disposed to adopt it, the British economic regime could never be integrally established in France. How then could one suppose that the parliamentary regime in France would be a faithful adaptation of Britain's?

But where has the British regime ever been able to establish itself fully economically and politically? The answer is not readily found. First, we can mention countries which certainly, in a fuller analysis, should not be lumped together—roughly, the Dominions. Their rural, commercial, and even their industrial conditions are close enough to those of Britain to explain the similarity.

Also, the countries of northern Europe, where agricultural skills have frequently treated small surfaces with technical perfection—horticulture, for instance. More generally, their commercial vocation as free exchange countries, limiting their activity to the food sector and only allowing for partial industries, is enough to bring out a certain correspondence with the social and political attitudes common to Britain. But here again a few distinctions are necessary: the Nordic parties do not have the cohesion of British parties.

There remains the United States. Indeed it is far from Europe by its geographical position and by its continental configuration. The distance explains the difference. As the British Empire was to be in the nineteenth century, so was the United States first an association of states, each one of which possessed self-government, grouped around a federal authority; but it was also an association of contiguous states linked first by roads, then railroads, and by currents of common interests. With time the federal tie became stronger. One of the elements strengthening this tie was the necessity of establishing protective tariffs against the powerful commercial and industrial traffic of the British, who prematurely dreamed, in the middle of the eighteenth century, of dominating North America. However, if the United States protected itself against Europe, the vastness of its own continent allowed it and incited it to practice a self-contained liberalism whose volume rapidly matched that of Europe and of its colonies. Thus, a majority of the different states tended toward an absolute liberalism of the British type within the framework of a federal republic, which for more than a century constituted an immense separate world. It is clear that the more the federation had to provide against European competition, the more the political character of the presidency of the United States moved away from the classic parliamentary tradition to take monarchical traits. But at this game the President risks clashes with the states, and the balance is at times barely re-established and only after weathering grave conflicts: a deep political and party reform was enough for Andrew Jackson, but Abraham Lincoln had to wage a bloody war. Franklin D. Roosevelt succeeded with the New Deal but had to leave untouched the federal structure. This should be enough to illustrate the difference between the American presidential regime and British parliamentarianism, enough also to elicit their resemblances. There was a slow evolution, typified in the election of the Presidents: what had first been conceived as a choice by an electoral college became a plebiscite. This evolution remained bound to respect the particular interests of the states when a British two-party system became rooted, to give a solid foundation to federal biparty government.

The North Atlantic region, with the British dominions, forms pre-eminently the region of more or less classic parliamentarianism. It is also the region where industrial progress has known complete success. There is a nearly perfect coincidence between parliamentary zones and zones of high living standards.

Let us come back to France. France tends toward a biparty parliamentary regime, but never quite achieves it, remaining much farther from it than does the United States. In reality there are two Frances. One is composed of big and medium-sized farms, of great metallurgical industries, of great textile and chemical industries. There progress has cleared matters enough for the political temperaments to resemble those characteristic of North Atlantic countries—and to accept the requirements of the two-party system. In the other France technical progress makes its way laboriously, often bringing more hardships than riches. The second one is even more varied than the first one and it deserves further discussion.

XIV

The Accidents of Progress: Eastern Continents and Southern Seas

MECHANIZATION and the rational exploitation of agriculture, commerce and industry first proved their value in England. By 1780 they had won their case; after a few very successful experiments the whole nation began transforming. This transformation brought with it a reversal of the traditional ratio between city and country populations. Eighty per cent rural in the seventeenth century, the population of twentieth-century England tends to become 80 per cent urban. The 50 per cent mark was reached about 1830 (see Figure 1).

The new technical and social organization passed from England to the continent. Did it progress gradually from west to east? Approximately, if, allowing for an inevitable margin of error, we consider the first symptoms of the phenomena of transformation. But let us beware. The geographical and historical complexities of Europe have rendered certain regions much more permeable to new structures than others. A typical example is Germany. Until about 1830 Germany kept its old look, wrapped up in feudalism, divided into little courts that dressed according to the most antiquated fashions. Politics and economics still wore a wig. No doubt about it, technically France was far ahead. Twenty years later Germany had caught up. After twenty more years Germany had passed France. And twenty years later still German technique almost matched Britain's, which in its anxiety moved closer to France.

It was a lunge forward: in three generations Germany accomplished what took England more than ten generations. Why this extreme speed, perhaps even greater than that exemplified by America? The answer is in the discovery of a substratum which revealed its prodigious wealth as soon as movement had scratched the surface of dead routine. The commercial vocation of this astonishing continental crossroads of Eurasia was hidden for centuries: it had not participated in the great oceanic conquests and, though it had known a partial activity, thanks to important road construction three centuries earlier, it was the railroads which at last gave it new horizons. Germany's development sucked central European trade northward, profiting tardily but handsomely from the displacement of the commercial center of gravity from the Mediterranean to the North Sea and the Baltic. This attraction to the north weakened Austria, master of the Mediterranean approaches, to the advantage of Prussia, guardian of the new accesses to the sea. German progress was not favored, as was America's, by operating on virgin territory. It developed on a territory encumbered by traditions, inner frontiers, particularisms, and nationalism—in short, by an infinity of psychological barriers. Led by Prussia, Germany nearly succeeded in unifying the truly German territories and in renewing its agriculture to the point of approximating England's accomplishments. But misfortune began when the German economic machine, equipped with a powerful motor and weak brakes, ran into frontiers. Austria gave way easily, but with France, England, Russia, and the United States the collision was violent; the machine exploded, killing millions.

The German political regime? It had a British type of economy and a British type of regime; actually, Germany practicing economic liberalism tended toward parliamentary liberalism. But the effort at internal unification was more American than English; or, better, it was typically continental—whence the brutality of the regime under the Iron Chancellor, the Empire, the dictatorship. It is a regime characterized by violent, spectacular, murderous catastrophes.

Italy enjoyed the unique superiority of having been urbanized and commercialized long before any other European land. This was thanks to the old Mediterranean trade which recovered a bit of its ancient primacy toward the end of the Middle Ages. Then the trade centers moved north. Poor in industrial wealth, Italy reached a standstill. It took quite an effort to regroup its little Renaissance principalities into a state commensurate with the railroad age. A similarity of needs and intentions, if not, alas, of means, associated Italy with Germany; this was despite the fact that Italy's relative industrial poverty created conditions more naturally comparable to those existing in France. Cavour had to face heavier tasks than Napoleon III did; more effective than the latter, he was less so than Bismarck. The structure of Italian society reached a modern urban stage of development faster than that of France, but for historical rather than technical reasons. As for the political regime, it tended toward a British type of parliamentarianism interrupted by catastrophes of the German type.

It is not easy to offer a short, clear definition of the analogies which bind Latin nations from the Mediterranean to the Pacific.

Their urban vocation manifested itself early: Peru, Mexico, and other pre-Columbian urbanization, Italy, Spain (as well as the Morocco of the Almoravides and of the Almohades); but they were not very permeable to nineteenth-century industrialization. At an ancient date their agriculture was wealthier and more perfected than anywhere else in the Western world; however, it was too rooted in old customs to lend itself easily to the British type of land reforms except in the deserted regions of South America (parts of Brazil, Uruguay, Argentina). Hence there too we observe a tendency toward an English type of parliamentary regime, but this tendency is frequently broken up by the anxious yearning of the masses looking for a supreme arbiter capable of restraining the ambitions of great capitalistic interests and capable of enforcing a respect for the old rural and urban traditions which new progress so cruelly threatens. From Mexico City to Buenos Aires, from Rome to Madrid, the periodic call on a *caudillo* stems from a chronic illness that reveals a temperament molded by permanent geographical and human imperatives.

The people (this vague word suits the summary character of our analysis) aspire to progress; of course they do. But not at the price paid by England: abolition of small rural property, complete and unsheltered risks assumed by industry and commerce. In Latin countries progress was accompanied by a period of parliamentary development. When the going became rough, Caudillo Rosas was called upon in Buenos Aires, more than a century before Franco. (Today in North Africa the Moroccan Democratic Party needs the monarch Mohammed V; and the Western-educated Habib Bourguiba, a man of middle-class birth, clashes with Salah ben Youssef, an Arab flattering religious and feudal traditions. In the meantime Syria is torn between military dictatorship and parliamentarianism.)

Finally, let us turn to the Slavic countries. There we do not find very much in the way of commercial and urban traditions—except perhaps in the zones contiguous to the great trade routes of the Tourana-Mongolian steppes. Old Slavic rural traditions are contrary to those in Latin countries, as far removed as possible from the notion of property handed down by Roman law. Willy-nilly, in spite of the Slavophile intentions of their reformers, the Slavic countries, and particularly Russia, followed from 1850 to 1917 the path of parliamentary capitalism. This orientation was in harmony with a very real and, in certain regards, an already gigantic effort to found factories, railroads, cities, and modern rural units. But here the task was too arduous, the traditions too deeply entrenched. The masses, having long kept a blind confidence in the czars, transferred it enthusiastically to a dictatorship, which can justly proclaim itself proletarian since it was born of the powerlessness of the English methods of liberal capitalism. It was in England that Marx had studied and denounced the faults, the weaknesses, of that liberal capitalism. The faults and weaknesses were not such, however, as to push England to Marxism. Yet how readily one understands Lenin's enthusiasm for Marx, whose criticisms offered a luminous explanation for the obvious insufficiencies of capitalism in Russia.

So much for our world survey. We do not mention the Far East, since it was, comparatively speaking, outside the sphere of Western progress until a recent date.

Now to come back to France. We stated earlier that an important part of the nation sullenly refused the British political processes because it could not completely adapt the corresponding modes of agricultural and industrial work. We must now consider this aspect of France in the light of the world's situation.

A great fraction of France is of continental structure. Until a very recent time a large portion of her agriculture was Germanic in structure. Surviving traits of the Germanic agrarian structure were even more evident in Lorraine before 1939 than in the heart of Germany. More than the proud vanity of Bismarck or the debility of Napoleon III, this inheritance from the high Middle Ages explains the catastrophic destiny of Alsace and Lorraine. Is the population of these two provinces French at heart? Absolutely—just as the men of Weimar in 1920 and those of Bonn in 1945 were sincere parliamentarians—but their feet are firmly planted in a land that looks eastward. Hence the loyal parliamentary character of northeastern France; but hence also a constant desire to escape disputes that might destroy national unanimity. This explains the movement for autonomy in Alsace and Lorraine to avoid their local destiny being dependent on political convulsions from the west or on wars from the east. The patriotic and religious shrines of the two provinces, the blast furnaces of the Moselle, the bleak landscape of the Haute-Marne, measure all the better the perils of German cataclysms because the technique, the industrial and urban progress, of these regions is of a Rhenish type: Mulhouse as well as Krefeld and Elberfeld has beaten England in many branches of the textile industry; the local steel mills, better equipped than England's, are a match for many Westphalian mills; and large farms are the rule in the departments of the Marne and the Haute-Marne.

It is rather difficult to give precise limits to a physical and moral territory that is so unique in the general French picture, a territory that is all the more exacting in its nationalism in that it fully realizes the power of German industry. Do the Ardennes, the Marne, and the Haute-Saône belong to it? Let us simply say that a rather large strip of territory marks the transition from the maritime style of western France to the continental type of eastern France.

And then in the Southeast. The bonds that link the old silk industry of the region of Lyons to the Milanese plain are too well known for us to belabor the subject. What about the Dauphiné (Isère, Hautes-Alpes, Drôme)? All of its mountain industry and agriculture resembles Italian industry: it tries to compensate for a lack of coal by a thorough exploitation of hydraulic power. Alpine industry is technical; it supports a type of population whose basic motivations and reactions are those of its neighbors to the east, south, and west. Marseilles has more affinities with Genoa than with Rouen. Orchards, vegetable and flower gardens, olive trees, and vineyards bear the same intimate mark of human culture on either side of the Franco-Italian Mediterranean border.

If we follow the Mediterranean westward, the transition from Italian to Spanish style is so gradual that it has no clear boundaries. There is little or no racial consciousness. The Italians settle down in the Garonne Valley and very rapidly espouse the political attitudes of the region; the same is true of them in Lorraine or Flanders. In Paris the Spanish lose little time in becoming Parisians. Therefore, a map of Spanish and Italian immigrations would be of little assistance in our analysis of French peculiarities: France cannot be defined by race, but only by conditions of life. Similar living conditions invite us to link this piece of France to Italian structures and reactions, that piece to Spanish structures and reactions. Yes, living conditions are the important element, not race. In any case, the *département* of the Basses-Pyrénées is above all a parcel of the Basque country which, monarchist at heart, straddles France and Spain. Even the community of life and methods of the "smuggling industry" along the Pyrenees serves to bring the rural and urban activities of France and Spain closer together.

And what is meant by "Mediterranean borders"? The religious faith, both Protestant and Catholic, of the Cévennes range, (mainly in Hérault and Gard) has its counterpart in Italy and Spain. As a matter of fact, we would be inclined to incorporate in the same zone the *départements* of Aveyron and Lozère. Once more we note a wide zone of transition between South and North, wider perhaps than between the east and the west of the Parisian region.

In the South political psychologies are typically Mediterranean. First there is a rather natural leaning toward extremes, rendering the stability of parliamentary customs difficult. The general inclination toward extreme positions often stands out more strongly than any specific attachment to the Right or the Left: a violent extreme Right is capable of attracting extreme leftists, who find their own leaders too moderate; inversely, the same movement may carry impatient rightists to the extreme Left. Of course, the parliamentary mentality finds a much more favorable terrain in the cities, particularly in the great trading centers between Nice and Toulouse.

Now let us turn to the most original of the French regions, those facing the Atlantic between the *départements* of the Manche and the Landes (in Brittany, Ille-et-Vilaine and Côtes-du-Nord can, in certain ways, be associated with Anglophile Normandy). There again a few great cities, Bordeaux, Nantes, and Poitiers, show themselves permeable to the political and economic psychologies characteristic of the North Atlantic. But the same can be said of Buenos Aires, Santiago of Chile, or Rio de Janeiro; for those isolated French urban pockets are surrounded by vast rural districts (which parenthetically owe many of their crops to plants originating in South America: tobacco, corn, potatoes), rural districts were, for lack of natural resources, industrial progress has always been difficult. In a certain measure, one can even state that industrialization there has failed to remain true to the promises held by the old industries of monarchical France (see Figure 3). As in Latin America small islands of the iron industry have managed to survive, but they have survived only thanks to international trade. On both sides of the South Atlantic we notice a like attachment to *métayage* (a form of sharecropping). The religious attitude generally reveals an active faith that deeply permeates social life (in Brittany, Vendée), but there are also manifestations of sincere rationalistic agnosticism. Auguste Comte, the single most powerful inspiration in the political evolution of Brazil, was born in Montpellier, and in the law school of Montpellier were trained many of the jurists who later founded the law schools of South America.

The political attitudes of the Atlantic regions, difficult to analyze in France, are often reproduced on a much larger scale in South America, where the very magnitude of their continental proportions facilitates analysis.

Of all the French Atlantic phenomena made clearer, more explicit by their exaggerated counterparts in Latin America, one must insist on the presence of a political temperament which we shall call, for lack of a better term, skill in compromise. The best word to describe this particular variety of "compromise" is Portuguese, *jeito*, and it has become an institution in Brazil under the name of "moderating power." This skill at compromise is made necessary by the rough schooling that political life offers in those countries: laicism versus clericalism and violent unsubmissiveness versus submissiveness to the landowners create irreducible theoretical oppositions. Nevertheless, technical equipment remains relatively limited; there are rather few cities; the bourgeoisie is more devoted to commerce than to industry; and concrete progress is infinitely slow, quite out of proportion with the absolute character of the political proclamations. The gap between theoretical positions and practical applications is such that, on the plane of action, adjustments have to be made between elements categorically opposed on the plane of ideas. It becomes an absolute necessity to seek reconciliation in parliament, even after apparently irreconcilable electoral ideologies have been adopted. It is this very phenomenon which maintained the imperial house of Bragance in power throughout the nineteenth century and which replaced it by presidents of the republic, whose artful suppleness would make even French Radical-Socialists look like clumsy apprentices. If a spurt of industrialization or modernization occurs, the moderating power contracts, leaving greater room to the old opposition between partisans of a classic parliamentary regime (loyal to the balanced left-right swing) and partisans of extremist regimes from the right or the left. In such cases, the major preoccupation of the spirit of compromise is to reconcile the various center fractions and pit them against both extremes: in the name of national solidarity it plays the role of a parliamentary watchdog. Once the crisis has waned (since the works of Simiand we know that economic crises and accelerated technical progress are simultaneous phenomena), parliamentary and antiparliamentary Left move back closer to one another, as do the parliamentary and the antiparliamentary forces of the Right; the moderating power immediately rushes to the help of the weaker of the two coalitions, inclining rightward in a predominantly Leftist country, inclining leftward in a predominantly Rightist country. Just as the South American elector cannot affirm that his candidate will remain the leftist or the rightist that he was during the campaign, so the French elector would be foolhardy to wager that his Radical-Socialist representative will remain faithful to the Right or to the Left for any length of time. Sensitivity to the concrete realities of government will oblige the Radical-Socialist to abandon ideological positions. Let a crisis reappear and he will once again be the hero of reconciliation and the defender of parliamentary survival, which, after all, is his outstanding quality.

FIGURE 17. Radical Votes and Abstentions in 1928 (*upper*); Socialist Votes and Abstentions in 1956 (*lower*).

Horizontal lines—abstentions more than 17% of the registered voters; R—Radicals more than 35%; S—Socialists more than 20%.

Though offering in the North the aspect of a leftist element in a two-party system, radicalism in 1928 and socialism in 1956 became, in the South, the center defenders of a rather unpopular parliamentary regime. Such is the role befitting a moderating power.

THE ACCIDENTS OF PROGRESS

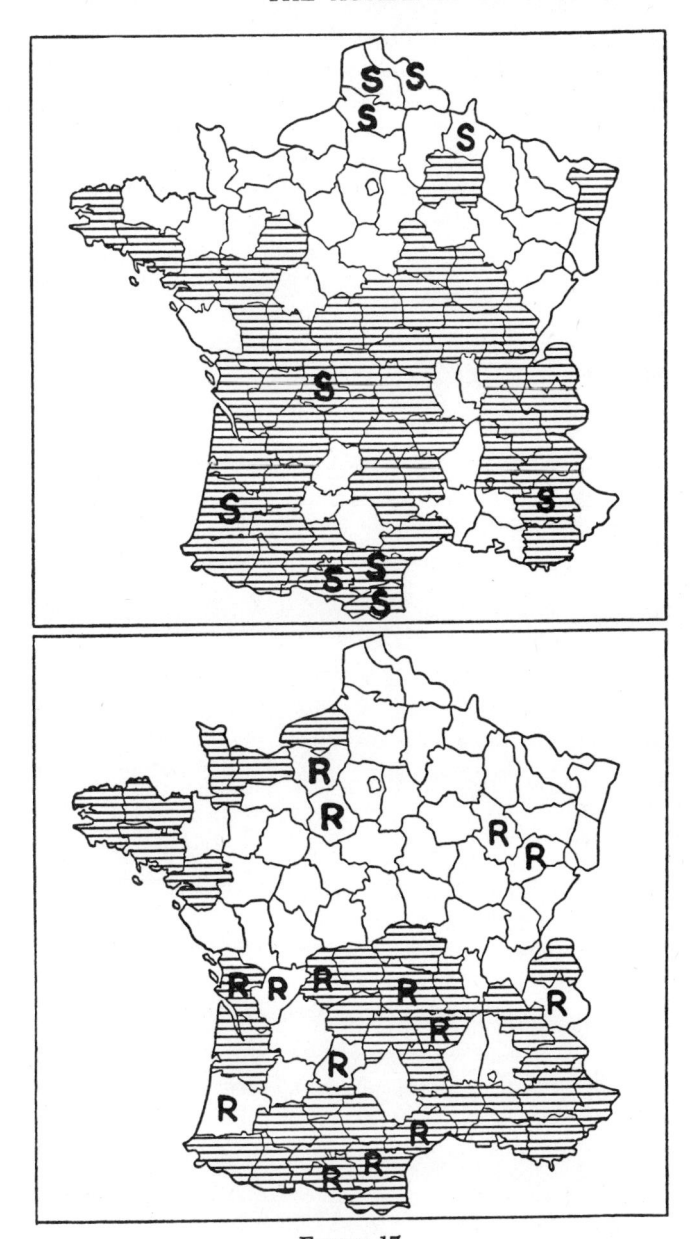

Figure 17

In France the exact extent of this large Atlantic zone is just as hard to measure on the north—where Ille-et-Vilaine and Côtes-du-Nord evince a more orthodox parliamentarianism—as on the south—where the Languedoc region, though habitually associated with Atlantic behavior, switches in time of crisis to the typical Mediterranean regime of a violent struggle of extremes that practically nullifies the moderating power's capacities.

Is the moderating power specifically Latin? In a certain measure, yes. Of course, there exists in Britain the counterpart of the "floating" votes. It is they who confer power, at times to Labour, at times to the Conservative Party. But these stray votes form no party of their own; fickleness is their virtue. The floating voter of the Latin type, on the contrary, expresses himself within the framework of an elastic party to which he remains fundamentally faithful —a faithfulness conditioned by the party's determined stand, come what may, as *the* center party. Such is the ambition of the moderating power in Brazil, an ambition quite alien to the Anglo-Saxon conception.

Our survey of France has not exhausted all aspects of her political diversity. There remains a compact and original center made up of the Massif Central (Puy-de-Dôme, Loire, Haute-Loire, Cantal, Corrèze, Haute-Vienne, Creuse, Indre, Cher, Nièvre, Allier). The Massif Central was a great industrial region under the Old Regime; it remained so during a great part of the nineteenth century. In the twentieth century it became the great victim of accelerated technical progress. The fragility of its industrial vocation proved fatal. The problem of communications was vital: once the local resources had been exhausted, central France could survive only if her highways and railroads were intensely developed. In fact, this development was never completely achieved; after 1860 there was a confidence in the industrial future of a region of diminishing resources. These conditions, also prevailing in many parts of Russia, were precisely those denounced by Lenin—obstacles in communications being the constant concern of Soviet planners. The relative isolation, on suddenly unfavorable soil, of regions whose psychological vocation was traditionally industrial provoked violent clashes. In fact, great landed property, less dependent than industry on communications, transformed itself in central France according to the British pattern. Is that the reason why extremist movements are so powerful in Berry (Cher, Indre)? And has not the presence of great state-owned factories there simply reinforced the cause of the extremists? Is that why regional communism made an early appearance in the district? Is that why this regional brand of communism has been extending to the southwest rather than toward the Saône and the Rhone valleys better supplied in railroads? Probably so.

Is central France the only "chosen" ground of communism? François Goguel has marked out two other zones long receptive to the extreme Left: the North (Ardennes and Aisne) and the South (the Mediterranean coast line). With regard to the Mediterranean coastal strip, we have already mentioned its propensity for extremism; it is ideal ground for a communism that can also move northward across Vaucluse to the sterile Lozère. With regard to the North proper, we should take notice that the economic destiny of the Ardennes rather resembles that of Berry; the recent gains of communism in the Vosges, a district undergoing a crisis of industrial readaptation, is a phenomenon of a like order confirming our hypothesis.

Perhaps these two prongs of Communist development

to the north and to the south might be considered the extension in France of two great natural axes of the Slavic world's destiny. Two great roads of transcontinental trade from China to Europe used to lead to the Mediterranean through the Balkans and to the Baltic through Poland. Starting with the eighteenth century, the slowing down and then the stopping of this great trade, the withdrawals and reversals which it caused in Eurasian Russia, appear an important element in the proletarian destiny of the countries concerned. After 1944 these two axes help the advance of communism. In northern and southern France French communism can be considered a geographical extension of world communism.

This closes our survey, which should not lead to the conclusion that France is a mere juxtaposition of stray pieces in a political puzzle. Such a notion would make any understanding of the basic French mechanisms impossible. For France was certainly the first country in the world to call forth the idea of national unity.

XV

France, Strength and Weakness of the World

LET us consider again per capita income. Once more France stands out as a crossroads, a crossroads of living standards. The distribution of per capita income discloses the existence of wealthy zones comparable to England's most prosperous districts (the Parisian region, the Rhone *département*), of a North close to the British proletariat type, of an East typically Germanic, of a Southeast belonging to the wealthier Italian type, and in the Atlantic zone of two important groups of *départements* whose living standards somewhat resemble those of the Latin world (southern Italy, Spain, and South America).

But in fact in nearly every region of France there exists a complete gamut of income types, as well as marks of every attitude and every political psychology. The only value of the pieces of the puzzle previously described is to bring out, with due allowance for necessary simplifications, the dominant characteristics of each region.

There is a French miracle. Germany is Germany, Italy

THE FRENCH AND THE REPUBLIC

is Italian, England is English, France is made up of pieces of the world, in any case of pieces of Europe. It is for that precise reason that France is France. To travel only from Lille to Metz, from Dunkerque to the Rhone, amounts to the same as taking the long trip from Manchester to Ludwigshafen, from Hull to Genoa. This is possible because France is such an amazing crossroads. The fact has been stated so many times, in so many ways, that the strangeness of the situation no longer strikes us. Yet this strangeness immediately comes to mind when, traveling outside France, one hears an Englishman vaunt the charm of his own South, meaning Brighton! As for Germany's South, it is Bavaria! On the other hand, the Spaniard or the Italian scarcely realizes what the North is like. Wherever he was born, a foreigner discovers familiar landscapes in France. There is less difference between Acapulco and Menton than between Menton and Besançon, less difference between Lodz and Tourcoing than between Tourcoing and Nantes. In the same way the French psychology is such that, in whatever part of the world he may be (except for the Far East and even then!), a Frenchman understands others and is understood by others. Characteristic traits of his culture and of the genius of his country allow him to make direct contacts with foreign worlds. It is a well-established fact, also, that the Frenchman is happy only in France; he repatriates as quickly as feasible. For what attracts to France and is found nowhere else is not a *specific* trait of French culture, but the coexistence of traits belonging to every culture. Coexistence? Certainly; yet even better the organic synthesis of every culture. We described types of regions, stating that everywhere in France one could find representatives of all types. But more than that, in every Frenchman one uncovers elements which, according to obviously variable hierarchies, owe something to every typical region of France. A foreigner can never perfectly understand a Frenchman unless he has traveled widely throughout the world. The Jews, for instance, are the most rapidly assimilated by French culture.

France was the first nation formed as a nation. This near miracle, which seems to contradict the infinite diversity of strongly opposed tendencies, is an evident fact inscribed in the book of history. And if American popularizations have obliged France to share this distinction with Denmark, it is because they choose to forget that the old Denmark is not at all today's Denmark but the ancestor of three modern nations. This is not the place to give reasons for the early synthesis of France. Much more than the Avignonese, the foreign tourist is aware that at one time Avignon was Rome. The Savoyard peasant no longer realizes the honor the ducal family of Savoy paid him when it became the regent of Italy's destiny. In Alsace the memory of Germany is scarcely a threat any longer; and if Lille is proud of being Flemish, it is ardently French.

Clearly, every crisis that jolts the world pulls painfully at France's seams. In the last twenty years Spanish refugees have poured into the Southwest, British soldiers were stationed in the North, Germans settled in the East, and Italians in the Southeast. Suffering resulted, but there was no serious threat to national unity. Twice in recent history France has borne modifications in the frontiers of Alsace and Lorraine, but no rapid disarticulation in the psychology of the two provinces has ensued.

When many Frenchmen, and most of their deputies and ministers, are at every moment of political life torn be-

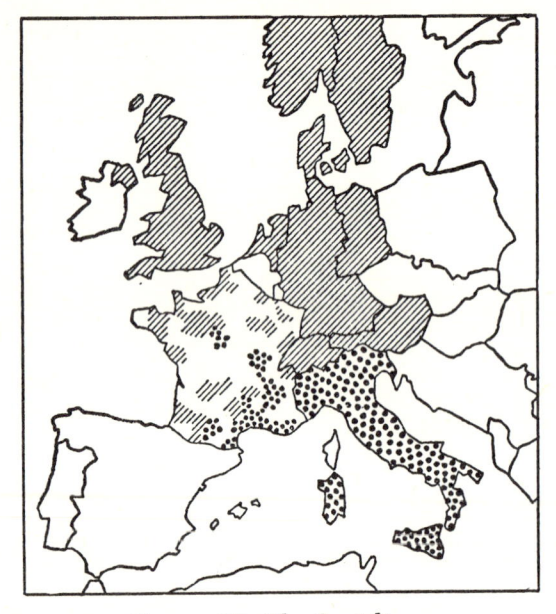

FIGURE 18. The Socialisms.

Lines—advances in northern countries; dots—regression in southern countries.

There are two types of socialism in Europe. In the Northwest and in central Europe, socialism is relatively unhampered by communism. There socialism was powerful before 1930 (about 30 per cent of the electorate). It has become even more powerful since 1944 (about 44 per cent). The French socialism of the North corresponds to this brand of socialism: strong before the war, it has progressed by only 3 per cent from 1928 to 1956. In southern Europe socialism was weaker; hard pressed by communism, it has lost ground since the war, with an over-all attrition of approximately 10 per cent from 1928 to 1956.

tween contrary tendencies, they are faithfully reflecting the psychological and political shocks of a modern world violently propelled by technical progress.

The political drama that dominates the world today is the opposition between East and West. Its effect on France

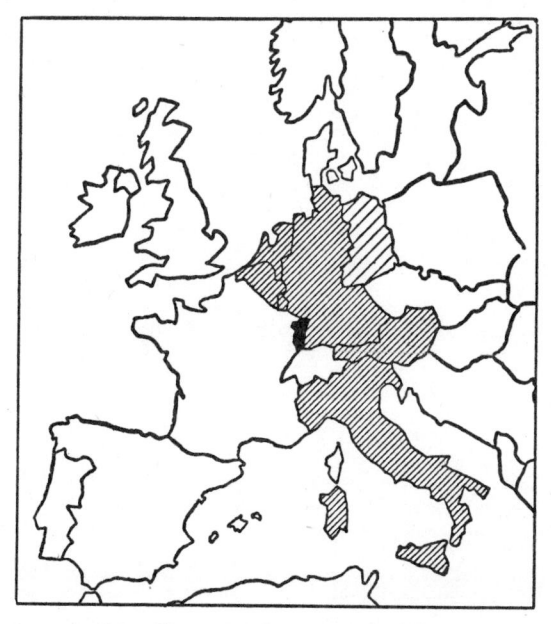

FIGURE 19. Christian Democratic Movements.

Close lines—zones of heavy concentration, in excess of 40% of the votes cast, before and after the war; black—MRP sectors with more than 30% of the votes in 1956.

In central Lotharingian Europe even before the war several more or less social-minded Christian parties had developed. In the same regions these parties emerged from the war considerably strengthened, obtaining more than 40 per cent of the votes. Before the war in France the *départements* of the Haut-Rhin and the Bas-Rhin were the seat of both autonomist and Christian movements. In 1956 these two *départements* were the only ones to give more than 30 per cent of their votes to the MRP.

is noteworthy. When a decisive break between America and Russia threatens, the mass of those who would feel inclined to come to the help of Russia is not composed merely of authentic Communists, of sympathizers, or of inhabitants of the zones previously described as favorable

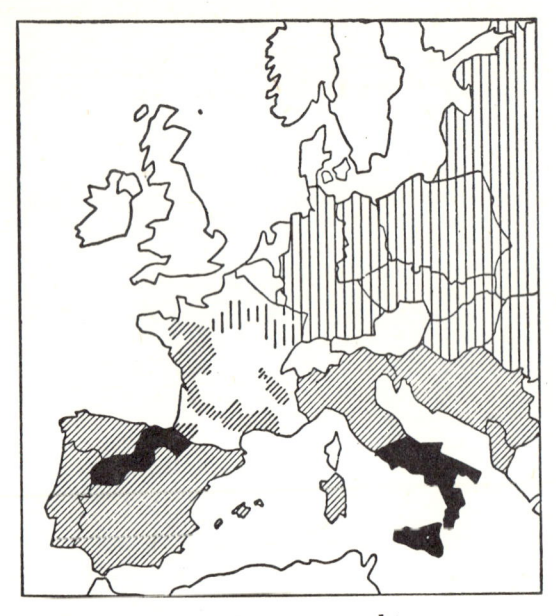

FIGURE 20. Dictatorships.

Vertical lines—countries of great industrialization, the North; diagonal lines—countries traditionally agricultural, the South; black—regions faithful to monarchy.

It is a delicate matter to propose a map of regions particularly inclined toward authoritarian regimes. Such a map must not be considered foolproof. In France we have placed under the category "Industry" some *départements* which are not normally oriented toward the right but which have given the RPF a relatively high number of votes. And we have linked to the typically latin *caudillo* regimes, the *départements* that gave Poujade most of his supporters.

to communism, for the Center Right and, above all, the extreme Right have numerous supporters who in such cases would speak the same language and follow the same line of action as the extreme Left. The extreme Left too exalts country and national independence.

What about the problem of European unity? The number of Frenchmen wholly committed to the ideal of European integration is certainly smaller than the number of Germans. This attitude is not easy for the foreigner to understand, but in the heart of the great majority of Frenchmen, even of the Frenchmen who refuse the idea of European integration, there is beside a big *No,* a *yes,* a small *yes* that fosters doubt. Thus, whatever the problem, France's reaction is made of many hues.

France, weakness of the world? She is said to be unstable. On the contrary, she is stability incarnate. All that is France reflects every degree, every shading; therein lies her originality.

Let us take the problem of technical progress. Although living standards in Russia may appear inferior to those of the North Atlantic nations, it is probable that the acceleration will be extremely rapid. In any event, seen from the sole point of view of modernization, the immense Russian complex deserves to be placed on an equal footing. Thus there may develop a single bloc of northern countries. France would then cease to be a point of balance between East and West, while remaining so between North and South. She would have to share this privilege with many bordering countries. It is the present triple position of France which makes for her originality. Let her lose one of these elements, what then could she pride herself on by comparison, say, with India, which is so much wealthier in manpower and whose industrialization is advancing rapidly?

France has been the world's microcosm. She can only remain so if her technical progress follows the scale of world progress. If not, France will fall to the rank of tomorrow's colonized nation—colonized by the Northeast or the Northwest but, in any case, by the North. On the other hand, an equal danger awaits her—that technical progress may alter the singular qualities of the French synthesis.

Here we are at the very heart of our investigation. Two answers are possible.

France reigned as master of the West at the time of rural civilizations. She remained a prodigious world animator as the rural civilizations became urban civilizations. So much for past glories.

But France has not been totally conquered by urban progress. She continues to show marked reticence in the face of technical progress. Is this a sign of wisdom or of senility? Will France have led the world during its transitional period, and only during that period? Or rather, has not her leadership during this period taken root in order to blossom forth slowly and splendidly in the new era of world history?

XVI

Conclusion

THIS essay was written in the spring of 1956. Since then, the collective reactions of the French have kept to a path which could have been foreseen on the basis of her evolution over the last one hundred years. The French edition of this book was published with a jacket which predicted early war or revolution. Was this an oversimplification? After October 1956 French public opinion crystallized around the notion of war, and, as usual in such cases, attachment to the parliamentary regime weakened.

No logical explanation can justify the enthusiasm or the nationalistic exasperation which broke out in France at the time of the Suez incident and which has been kept alive by the situation in North Africa. It is probable that 70 per cent of the French nation experienced a feeling of relief and exaltation when it learned that its troops and ships were moving on Port Said and the Canal. This feeling was strong even in those who realized the deeply unreasonable character of the operations. It was a matter of the heart, not one of reason. This sort of unanimity profited one of the strangest governments the Republic has known—strange, not because of its program, but because of its relatively authoritarian character, authoritarian enough to infringe upon a few of the "essential" democratic liberties.

It would be easy—and numerous political writers have done so with brio—to compare the attitudes of the Socialists in power with various points of the program which they had previously submitted to their electors. But what is more striking yet is that the Socialist Party (and this is one of the parties in which leaders maintain close contact with the militants) approved by a large majority all of these breaches of promise. In short, France became angry. She is still angry. If international political structures were today what they were a century ago, one can well imagine that France might have started a war against Islam or run the risk of a war on the pattern of the Crimean campaign of 1854-1856.

We speak of international structures, and not of international conjunctures, because the international conjuncture was in fact favorable to such an operation as that of Suez. In 1956 Europe, just as France, was shaken by a violent need for renewal reminiscent of 1848-1850, a shock to which the rapid progress of technical equipment was not foreign, a shock capable of awakening old feelings— the Hungarian revolution. The fall of 1956 was a period of fever, such as France and Europe had experienced at nearly regular intervals over the last 150 years.

But Europe is no longer the summit of world structures. It is dominated by new powers; its political reactions are no longer arrived at in utter freedom but under international control. This international control, and all sorts of direct or hidden interventions, prevent Europe and particularly France from giving full expression to their reactions.

CONCLUSION

In this manner the Suez operation was blocked. And today the freedom of French action in North Africa, especially in Algeria, is strongly threatened.

Nothing is better able to bring out the new relatively subordinate position of Europe, which only yesterday enjoyed an aristocraticlike freedom, than the hesitant, incomplete character of its reactions. This situation is particularly applicable to France, yesterday the freest nation —and at times the most unreasonable, as we have so often recognized in this book—today, more disconcerted than any other by the new conditions of the world political scene.

The development of social structures in the France of today would deserve a thorough study. It would probably reveal a wider gap between classes, wider not so much by comparison with the situation in 1860 or 1890 (since the over-all increase in wealth has benefited the lower classes) as by comparison with 1945. This trend toward differentiation is possibly on the order of those occurring during the major French crises of the nineteenth century when the railways were being established.

The industrial motor of this crisis of exasperation is the acceleration in the development of energy and the speculations which it involves. Having spoken of the problems of Europe, the Orient, and Africa, we must complete the picture of contemporary French passions by mentioning the feverish search for oil. Once again, though it may not be as easy to exploit as many others, the French subsoil is not without resources. And once again it is only at a high degree of technical power that the difficult organization of French oil production can be arrived at. Metropolitan France is a latecomer poorly endowed for an oil economy, just as she was poorly endowed for a coal economy: the similarities in the social reactions caused by these two economies are striking.

The problems confronting France in the Sahara are not new ones. On the historical plane we pointed out how the extension of French occupation to the hinterlands was bound both to a singular French vocation for continental expansion and to the difficulty encountered in maintaining coastal outlets. The political cycles which we observed in the case of French possessions in India and America in the eighteenth century and in Africa in the nineteenth century can serve as models for France's present strength and weakness in North Africa. France is master of the Sahara, as she was of the interior of India and North America before the development of non-French shipping and trading companies cut her off from home. No economic or political power can contest (by war or law) France's right to the Sahara. But what will become of her Saharan outlets? Are we going to witness that cutting off from the ports which so frequently recurs in France's destiny? Everything is in place for a repetition of this situation.

Of course, the foreign intervention of capitalistic powers, better fitted than France to equip and organize trade in the great North African ports, has not manifested itself as openly as in India, America, or Atlantic Africa. But at heart the problem remains the same: Will France's technicians, matériel, and capital suffice to preserve French political authority on the shores of the Mediterranean as well as along the supply lines toward the interior? This is the essential question.

The importance of these maritime outlets is so great that one readily understands France's tenacity in Algeria. But there, too, the old French style is evident. At the very mo-

CONCLUSION

ment when an enormous technical effort is imperative, France turns her energy toward military operations. At a time when industry should be mobilizing all the nation's human resources, France is engaged in a war. It is but another case of Bonapartism. Of course, we do not deny the very great progress accomplished by French industry in the last twenty years, and more particularly in the last few years. Still, one questions whether this effort, so significant in relation to the internal French situation, is great enough to meet France's needs in Africa, great enough to meet the progress of competing nations.

Logically—but politics has little in common with logic—it is paradoxical that France should expend so much energy in military operations on the very continent where she ought to be mustering every effort in order to equip her Africa (French Africa; or simply Africa, the friend of the French; or even only the regions friendly to France). The same logic would require that France learn the language and the customs of the Arabs and also teach the techniques of modernization to its 400,000 draftees rather than teaching them the military techniques of the present program of pacification. But it is absurd to expect logic in this domain. Nations as well as men live according to their passions, not according to their reason. France, Lamartine said a hundred years ago, is a bored nation. As we have tried to point out, she is today rather an irritated nation. And she is irritated, even while achieving one of the greatest technical advances of her history, at observing that this advance remains inferior to her needs and to her merits. In 1956–1957, in 1848–1854, in fact all the time, irritation has been the cause of French political crises.

Whence the following situation, equally paradoxical: At a time when she forcefully proclaims her exclusive rights in

North Africa, demonstrating a spirit of courage and sacrifice, France also requires urgent foreign technical assistance. We should not be surprised at an attitude more juridical than rationally economic; it is a basic French trait. From this position stems the vigor with which France pretends to need no one in the military or political realm while recognizing the need for many friends in the technical, commercial, and financial realm. Her need of dollar and other foreign loans, her own hidden gold assets, would not be too serious in themselves, were it not proof of her dependency on foreign powers at the precise moment when she expects of these same powers a rigorous policy of noninterference in French affairs.

Today, as happened so often during the last 150 years, we are led to cry out: "If only we were wealthier!" Why did nature endow us with so many virtues—mind you, reader, it is a Frenchman who speaks!—while refusing us the material means of applying them?

This old contradiction is so fundamentally French that it explains how the Socialist Party has been able to practice its present policies without the slightest fear of being accused of infidelity or inconsistency. While it should have committed itself to a radical transformation of France's economy and of her international relations, the Socialist Party seems to believe that it has accomplished a great deal by establishing old-age retirement and by launching on paper a plan for socialized medicine. Doubtless the Socialist Party realizes that it is powerless to modify significantly the temperament of the French people, a necessary condition to any permanent reform.

We shall not insist any longer on the illogical, though well-founded French passion that demands total independence of political action while clamoring for a complete

CONCLUSION

solidarity of the world's economies. This stubbornly juristic point of view arises from a strictly French nineteenth-century conception of liberty.

Nevertheless, we shall conclude here on the same note that we might very well have adopted a year ago: the re-education of a nation's passions represents a long effort and the same is true of the necessary technical re-education. Just how advanced is the educational effort? For better than ten years now the plan for educational reform has been stagnating, constantly cut or altered in some fashion by one minister after the other. Every new government inscribes it as an essential part of its program; yet for diverse reasons it is always being postponed. Generally it is considered too costly, even though its cost is only the equivalent of a few months of military operations, and the military as well as the civilian future of the nation depends on it. Here again the governments themselves are less to blame than the temperament of the whole people. Can the reform of France's education be achieved only in the throes of a great internal crisis? Or will it be achieved through a conversion of the national temperament under the pressure of the world situation?

The key to the French predicament of 1958 seems to be the following: Either a violent crisis will bind France around a leader, as so often has been the case in her history, thereby isolating her from the world that she may better direct her energy to exclusively national tasks, or else world co-operation will have acquired enough strength to bring about, not so much a change of political attitudes through constraint, as a relative change of temperament through the realization that international ties in the twentieth century are firm enough to deflect and correct passions inherited from the nineteenth century.

This hesitation between two possible courses explains the gravity and the length of the governmental crisis in the fall of 1957. The world remains deeply divided. The fact appears less in the resounding technological rivalry opposing Russians and Americans than in the obscure but decisive actions which pit the two sides against each other in the Middle East. There, while Americans and Russians vie to win the favors of the Arabs, the French are defending Europe's position with the help of Israel in the Arab world of the Orient and in Algeria at the heart of the Arab world of the West. In accordance with their ancestral passions, the French are defending these positions less by economic activity—toward which they have preserved their old inferiority complexes and an atavistic anxiety that breeds contempt for "business"—than by diplomatic action and particularly military action, for which France's youth lets itself be mobilized more readily than to recast obsolete rural structures or build new cities. This military action, undertaken with relatively outmoded methods and possible because the enemy's are even more so, is significant because it stresses the real courage of the troops: obviously, no one will accuse young Frenchmen of having left their fields, their shops, or their factories out of material interests. Never rapidly decisive, military action in Algeria has awakened distrust in both East and West; at the same time it has stopped, or at least has severely slowed down, a French economy which begins to feel the need of assistance from the West and perhaps even from the Eastern bloc. Once more France lives tragic hours.

In the fall of 1957 a rightist majority was impossible in the National Assembly; this became evident in the face of Antoine Pinay's failure to form a cabinet. A leftist majority was equally impossible, as was borne out by Guy Mollet's

CONCLUSION

failure. Hence the government reverted once again to the Center in the person of Félix Gaillard, a member of the Radical-Socialist Party.

But that party is now split into rightist and leftist wings. The split has been strong enough to create rather spectacular withdrawals, reducing the number of Radical deputies from fifty-four to forty-three. And within the ranks of this depleted party various bitter divisions exist. It will appear somewhat paradoxical that this small party should be called upon to furnish both the head of the government (Gaillard) and the leader of the opposition (Mendès-France). In order to survive their internal divisions the Radicals chose Daladier as party president; he proved all the more acceptable in that any new political initiative on his part appears completely out of question so long as public opinion remembers the unhappy days of 1939–1940. In order to act the same party brought to the fore one of its youngest members, Félix Gaillard, who had no political past to justify. As the leader of a majority rather than as the promoter of a policy, he assumed the role of a pilot steering a ship without a course, simply hoping to save the vessel from the currents that push it along.

Today France's fate is being decided by forces at large in the world. Caught between a young socialism already undergoing revision and an old capitalism still being revised, the ship of France tosses in heavy seas. If France no longer guides the world, she preserves the privilege of being the example of the world's conflicts. Beyond the good will or the programs of the statesman who leads her, the fate of France will inform the peoples of the world whether they can expect to move toward a renovated socialism or a renovated capitalism, toward a world conflict or toward a few decades of peace.

There have been periods when France lavished advice and provided the world with examples and theories. Today France is silent; she offers contradictory examples in the name of contradictory principles. But the keener political observers are not deceived by it all. The difficulties of France are the difficulties of the world. One may react to them with distress or with anger, in the same way as one might react at the sight of a barometer whose unforeseeable oscillations reflected the world's destiny.